MIKE BARTLETT

Mike Bartlett is a multi-award-winning playwright and screenwriter.

His plays include *Scandaltown* (Lyric Hammersmith, London); *The 47th* (The Old Vic, London/Sonia Friedman Productions/ Annapurna Theatre); *Mrs Delgado* (Arts at the Old Fire Station, Oxford/Theatre Royal Bath/Oxford Playhouse), *Snowflake* (Arts at the Old Fire Station/Kiln Theatre, London); *Albion* (Almeida Theatre, London, also filmed for BBC Four); *Wild* (Hampstead Theatre, London); *Game* (Almeida); *King Charles III* (Almeida/ West End/Broadway; Critics' Circle Award for Best New Play, Olivier Award for Best New Play, Tony Award nomination for Best Play); *An Intervention* (Paines Plough/ Watford Palace Theatre); *Bull* (Sheffield Theatres/Young Vic Theatre, London/ Off-Broadway; TMA Best New Play Award, Olivier Award for Outstanding Achievement in an Affiliate Theatre); *Medea* (Glasgow Citizens/Headlong/Watford Palace); *Chariots of Fire* (based on the film; Hampstead/West End); *13* (National Theatre, London); *Love, Love, Love* (Paines Plough/Plymouth Drum/ Royal Court Theatre, London; TMA Best New Play Award); *Earthquakes in London* (Headlong/National Theatre); *Cock* (Royal Court/Off-Broadway, Olivier Award for Outstanding Achievement in an Affiliate Theatre; revived in the West End); *Artefacts* (nabokov/Bush Theatre, London); *Contractions* and *My Child* (Royal Court).

Bartlett has received BAFTA nominations for his television series *The Town* (ITV) and *Doctor Foster* (Drama Republic/ BBC), for which he won Outstanding Newcomer for British Television Writing at the British Screenwriters' Awards 2016. His screen adaptation of his play *King Charles III* aired on BBC Two in 2017, and his other television series include *Life* (BBC One), *Sticks and Stones* and *Trauma* (both Tall Story Pictures for ITV), and *Press* (Lookout Point for BBC One). Bartlett has also written several plays for radio, winning the Writers' Guild Tinniswood and Imison Prizes for *Not Talking*.

Mike Bartlett

SCANDALTOWN

NICK HERN BOOKS

London

www.nickhernbooks.co.uk

A Nick Hern Book

Scandaltown first published in Great Britain in 2022 as a paperback original by Nick Hern Books Limited, The Glasshouse, 49a Goldhawk Road, London W12 8QP

Scandaltown copyright © 2022 Mike Bartlett

Mike Bartlett has asserted his right to be identified as the author of this work

Cover image: photography by Helen Maybanks, design by Matt Hodges

Designed and typeset by Nick Hern Books, London
Printed in Great Britain by Mimeo Ltd, Huntingdon, Cambridgeshire PE29 6XX

A CIP catalogue record for this book is available from the British Library

ISBN 978 1 83904 055 9

Scandaltown was commissioned by and first performed at the Lyric Hammersmith Theatre, London on 7 April 2022, with the following cast:

PHOEBE VIRTUE	Cecilia Appiah
JACK VIRTUE	Matthew Broome
AUNTY JULIE / REBECCA DE SOUZA	Emma Cunniffe
PETER MEDIA OBE / CARSON	Henry Everett
MATT ETON	Richard Goulding
FREDDIE PERIPHERAL	Luke Hornsby
TOM DOUBLE-BUDGET	Thomas Josling
HANNAH TWEETWELL	Aysha Kala
ROSALIND DOUBLE-BUDGET	Annette Mclaughlin
JENNY HOOD	Ami Okumura Jones
SIR DENNIS HEDGE / KEVIN THE POSTMAN	Chukwuma Omambala
LADY SUSAN CLIMBER	Rachael Stirling

Director	Rachel O'Riordan
Set Designer	Good Teeth
Costume Designer	Kinnetia Isidore
Lighting Designer	Paul Keogan
Sound Designer and Composer	Simon Slater
Choreographer	Malik Nashad Sharpe
Wigs, Hair and Make-up Designer	Susanna Peretz
Casting Director	Amy Ball CDG
Gender Consultant	Dr Lloyd (Meadhbh) Houston
Intimacy Director	Yarit Dor
Assistant Director	Kwame Owusu
Company Stage Manager	Claire Bryan
Deputy Stage Manager	Helen King
Assistant Stage Manager	Aiman Bandali

A Lyric Hammersmith Theatre production, presented in association with Fictional Company.

Characters

AUNTY JULIE, *forty-five, white, northern*
DOUBLES WITH
REBECCA DE SOUZA, *forty-four, white, posh, incredibly southern*

PHOEBE VIRTUE, *her niece, twenty-two, mixed heritage*

JACK VIRTUE, *her nephew, twenty-two, mixed heritage*

SIR DENNIS HEDGE, *fifty, black, very rich*
DOUBLES WITH
KEVIN THE POSTMAN, *forty, black, rustic*

FREDDIE PERIPHERAL, *twenty-two, white, southern*

JENNY HOOD, *twenty-four, East Asian, southern, British*

HANNAH TWEETWELL, *twenty-five, South Asian, southern, British*

LADY SUSAN CLIMBER, *forty-five, white, southern*

MATT ETON, *forty, white, southern, very posh*

PETER MEDIA OBE, *fifty, white, southern, Cambridge*
DOUBLES WITH
CARSON, *seventy, white, aged*

ROSALIND DOUBLE-BUDGET, *fifty, white, southern, Cambridge*

TOM DOUBLE-BUDGET, *her son, twenty-two, white, southern, sheltered*

Plus assorted PARTY GUESTS, *etc., played by the members of the company.*

Setting

Note on Text

(/) means the next speech begins at that point.

(–) means the next line interrupts.

(…) at the end of a speech means it trails off. On its own it indicates a pressure, expectation or desire to speak.

A line with no full stop at the end indicates that the next speech follows on immediately.

The play is set in 2022, performed in a proscenium arch theatre, in the style of a Restoration Comedy. Think painted backdrops, wings, asides, and refined props. Costumes should have the tension and flair of Restoration with the contemporary style and edge of Alexander McQueen. Everything should be joyful and fun.

This text went to press before the end of rehearsals and so may differ slightly from the play as performed.

ACT ONE

Scene One

The front garden of a cottage. The countryside. Morning.

AUNTY JULIE *comes out of her house, hungover, smoking, and on her phone. She puts some air-freshener on the wall.*

JULIE Ooo my head feels like it's been caved in with a pickaxe. She's been staying up late recently so it's been ages since I've had any fun. Last night I couldn't take it, so I went up to my bedroom, got under the covers with a bottle of Smirnoff and those jazz cookies you gave me, had a little party all on my own. It wasn't the best look, probably, but I had a fucking good time, and she was none the wiser, which is what matters isn't it, in the end?

Feeling rough this morning though. Just waiting for Kev. Only chance we get for a bit of it, first thing, back of his van before little madam gets up and –

PHOEBE (*From offstage.*) Aunty?

JULIE Oh shit – Call you back.

She hangs up, stubs out the cigarette. Sprays herself with air-freshener, takes a mint out of her pocket. Puts it in her mouth, and turns, just as PHOEBE VIRTUE *comes out of the house.*

PHOEBE Aunty! There you are! Here I am thinking I'm an early bird, ready to savour the rosy fingers of dawn, all prepared to pick herbs and surprise you in bed with a stimulating infusion, but when I get downstairs, I hear your voice, and you're out already! Let me embrace you!

JULIE Er. Alright.

She does.

PHOEBE   Ah! So fresh! Most people don't smell too good in the morning, but your benevolence means you sleep peacefully and wake as new, naturally fragrant with mint and juniper. But why are you out here? Doing the chores I suppose? The *bins*? Waving the community off to work, with a smile on your face and a click in your heel?

JULIE   Well er – yeah, you've got me. Thought I'd just... check

PHOEBE   You are the wisest, kindest aunt one could hope for. From the moment you took myself and my twin brother Jack in as babies on the death of our mother, you have raised us as your own, with never complaint or fatigue. You've done precisely as you pledged to our late mother – your sister – and brought us up the most virtuous, progressive and moral young people in the whole country.

JULIE   Don't I know it?!

PHOEBE   What's that Aunty?

JULIE   Oh er yes well – did my best!

PHOEBE   And in this hard, too-evil world, your best has been heaven. But alas, if only my night was so blissful. As you can tell from my zombie face, I struggled for sleep.

JULIE   You look alright.

PHOEBE   Bless you Aunty but I look *old*. Lines, bags – I look like *you*.

JULIE   Beg your pardon?

PHOEBE   You have no choice but to wear the disfiguring scars of time, but I'm only twenty-two.

JULIE   Didn't you put on your meditation whatsit?

PHOEBE   I did. But then at three in the morn, I awoke, eyes wide, in a complete state of panic.

JULIE   Was it that climate change again?

PHOEBE   Not this time. For since we've binned your plastic, given your car away, and stopped all your holidays I feel much better. No. It was my brother Jack. I'm concerned.

JULIE   Oh Jack's alright. He's like you. Since he left for London to volunteer for the RSPCA or whatever it was –

PHOEBE   Unicef Aunty.

JULIE   – all his messages have been telling us how he's doing really well, helping all those poor dogs –

PHOEBE   Children. Indeed, he was most regular in his messages – for we've always been inseparable – but the last two weeks, nothing. It isn't like him. The world is a terrible place, as you know, full of evil people like Andrew Neil. And those friends you used to have – I'm so glad we agreed to get rid of them all by the way.

JULIE   Hmm.

PHOEBE   You might be lonely now but it was a teachable moment. Anyway I worry Jack may have fallen in with the wrong company.

JULIE   Jack's a fine young man.

PHOEBE   But London is a strange place Aunty.

JULIE   Well yes so I've heard –

PHOEBE   On one hand it contains the most wonderous thinkers and activists! People I would so love to meet and talk to about how we can all make the world a better place! But on the other hand, there's people of your age – having affairs, making money, doing drugs, and only thinking of themselves.

JULIE   Yeah sounds really bad.

PHOEBE   So I worry, what if Jack forgot who he was?

JULIE   I'm sure he's fine.

PHOEBE Then why no message?

        KEVIN THE POSTMAN *enters*.

KEVIN   Hello there my kettle! Who's hot and steaming this
        morning? I reckon we've got ten minutes if you
        fancy a postman's knock in the back of the old –

JULIE   Oh morning postman who I don't know that well!
        I'm just here with my young niece Phoebe, who's
        up *unusually early*...

KEVIN   You – Oh. Right.

PHOEBE Oh sir! How wonderful it must be to have an
        occupation that starts the day with such energy!

KEVIN   Yes I appreciate a job first thing. Gets me up.
        Don't it Julie?

JULIE   Have you got anything to deliver *Mr Postman*?

KEVIN   Yes I've got quite a package here I was hoping to
        fit in your slot.

PHOEBE Oh for the days when people would get real letters!
        I'm too young to recall such a time but you must
        both remember. I write a lot of correspondence.

KEVIN   Do you?

PHOEBE There's nothing like it! You should always use a
        real pen, ensure it's full to the brim, then once
        you've given it a good workout, you take the
        resultant tome gently in your hand, move it
        towards the cover, insert it all the way inside,
        before using your tongue to softly lick the flap.
        What? Oh you both think that sounds like sex! It's
        so sad your lazy generation, raised in the
        disgusting 1990s, are so conditioned by a
        pornographic society. It's no wonder you have
        achieved so very little. Aunty, and Mr Postman,
        you should think about going on a course to
        reprogramme your exploitative associations.

KEVIN   I like the sound of her pornographic society. We should join that…

JULIE   Got any letters Kev?

He gets them out and gives them to AUNTY JULIE.

KEVIN   Aunty Julie…

He turns to PHOEBE.

And one for you. Phoebe Virtue.

She looks at it. KEVIN *turns back to* AUNTY JULIE.

See you tomorrow. Or, if you can't wait, come round mine. Got those handcuffs from Amazon. We could try them out. Let me know! Bye!

He goes. AUNTY JULIE *turns guiltily to* PHOEBE, *who is looking at her envelope –*

JULIE   I don't know what he was talking about! How disgusting! 'Amazon' indeed…

But PHOEBE *hasn't been paying attention.*

PHOEBE   Aunty it's from Jack! His handwriting! At last he's replied!

She opens the envelope, takes out the letter.

'Dear Phoebe, it's touching that you have such concerns about my life here in London. But be consoled I am the brother you always knew. Faithful, true, and always making sure I tread lightly, to leave the world a better place than whence I joined.'

He used the word 'whence'. Very reassuring.

'As you'll know from Instagram I'm working for Unicef but have recently supplemented this by helping out at the food bank at lunchtimes and in the evening I go on Twitter and call people out for being offensive. The work is important and humbling. Know that I think of you often sister. But trust me all is well. I will write again soon, Jack.'

Oh happy day! How silly of me! To believe he had fallen from the heavens and was there in the dirt, corrupted in the squalid –

She stops and looks at her fingers.

…squalid… But what's this… powder? It came out of the envelope. It's white –

JULIE White? Hang on. Why don't you give it here, I'll… check.

  PHOEBE *gives* AUNTY JULIE *the envelope. She looks in, seeing how much there is…*

PHOEBE Wait – there's a drug that's a white powder –

JULIE Is there?

PHOEBE Yes Aunty, you won't know but it's called cocaine. It must have accidentally fallen into the envelope when he posted the letter. But why has he got cocaine in his – Oh. And what's this… ink… on my finger, and here on the page…

  She holds it up.

  I hold it to the light. Some print. The letter must have been resting on something when it was written…

  Oh!

  She throws it away. AUNTY JULIE *retrieves it.*

JULIE What?

PHOEBE It cannot be believed!

  AUNTY JULIE *picks it up and tries to see.*

JULIE 'The… Tele… Graph.'

PHOEBE What dost my fair brother have a copy of that foul rag 'pon his desk?

JULIE   Oh... just chip paper, probably!

PHOEBE   Aunty, chip shops haven't used newspaper in
             decades. For who would want an inky fish? No the
             only thing wrapped in this murky epistle is my
             brother's hidden character.

JULIE   Oh, I'm sure it's just –

PHOEBE   London has done its work – corrupted my sibling
             from the solemn vow he made to honour our late
             mother's memory. Oh what would she say if she
             could see this now? Spinning in her grave like a
             wind turbine in an increasingly common weather
             event.

             PHOEBE *takes the envelope of cocaine from*
             AUNTY JULIE, *and holds it in one hand and the*
             letter in the other. AUNTY JULIE *edges to*
             retrieve the coke.

             Her beautiful son, reduced to snorting an ethically
             unforgivable drug, while reading such a
             reactionary rag as this.

JULIE   Yes, it's awful. Shall I just –

PHOEBE   I must save him from the clutches of the depraved
             metropolis. But if I arrive as I am, he will simply
             hide it, pretend to be my erstwhile virtuous
             brother. And that will not do. To remedy the boy
             I must know the full extent of his illness.

JULIE   You could just call him? He'd probably –

PHOEBE   I shall go to London and approach him in disguise.

JULIE   You – What?!

PHOEBE   – infiltrate his world and bravely set my eyes upon
             the ugly mutation. Once I'm satisfied I have the
             measure, I'll reveal myself, and seek the cure.

JULIE   You mean... You want to go to London?

PHOEBE   Aunty, I'm aware it's hard, but every moment
             wasted could spell his demise. I must pack.

JULIE   (*Excited.*) Wait – you mean… move out?

PHOEBE   Oh but Aunty – you're worried how you'll cope without me!

JULIE   (*Hurriedly.*) Oh. No, no –

PHOEBE   For you're so old, and frail.

JULIE   I'm forty-five.

PHOEBE   Exactly. Don't fret, I'll label the recycling bins.

JULIE   Nah you go love, I'll manage.

PHOEBE   You mean you think I should leave today?

JULIE   Why not this morning? Not a second to lose.

PHOEBE   Oh Aunty! So selfless. Well then. I must find a costume, and book a ticket for London forthwith.

        (*Aside.*) I must confess, despite my trepidation, I find the idea of such an adventure rather… bracing. To finally confront in person the very depravity I've only ever read about!

JULIE   You er…

PHOEBE   Yes Aunty?

JULIE   You want me to look after that powder for you? While you're away. Keep it safe, as evidence?

PHOEBE   Good idea. We don't want it falling into the wrong hands.

        She gives it over to AUNTY JULIE.

        Wish me fortune Aunty, adventure awaits!

JULIE   Bye!

        PHOEBE *goes.*

        AUNTY JULIE *dips her finger in the powder and snorts the coke. Enjoys, then runs offstage shouting –*

        Kevin! Come back! She's gone!

Scene Two

Jack Virtue's lodgings. East London.

The following morning.

JACK VIRTUE *enters in just his immaculate underwear, smoking a cigarette. He is unquestionably an Adonis.*

He stands proud.

JACK   By George, I feel unusually magnificent this morning. Glory has a name and that name is Hannah! Yes she well and truly took advantage of me. I can't remember everything we got up to, but I guess it was profound as my muscles have an Olympic ache and my tongue a noted stretch. Yes that was the kind of sex we'll be grateful to look back on when we're old and irrelevant. We'll say whatever I failed to do with my life, at least I got that night *right.*

                Enter HANNAH TWEETWELL, *putting the last of her clothes on.*

HANNAH   I enjoyed our intercourse. 'Twas most athletic. But now I must leave –

JACK   Pray why?

HANNAH   I attend an interview to work for Lady Susan Climber as her social media consultant.

JACK   By Jove you're brave! By reputation she is most fierce.

HANNAH   But she accounts for that ferocity with cash. And after her recent errors, she is most in need. So farewell…

                HANNAH *holds out her hand.*

                I beg your pardon but your name? In all our sweaty grapp'ling I never found what you were called?

JACK   Jack.

HANNAH   Good then Jack. Be nimble! And you certainly were.

            She turns to go.

JACK   Wait – Stay for breakfast! I need some exercise to work off my... hangover.

HANNAH   Jack really! I can't be seen in such a place as this.

JACK   Why not? It's bohemian.

HANNAH   Oh sir, you jest! It's a fucking disgrace. These omnipresent lice!

JACK   'Tis true but even so, we must meet once more! You would agree that when our bodies intertwined we produced an unusual amount of pleasure? For us to be separate would defy nature.

            She looks at him. She takes out a pen and paper. Writes something.

HANNAH   Hmm. Your character holds no interest for me, but sensually I can't deny 'twas a fullsome ride. I doubt they'll let you in, but if you can find entry tonight, I shall be here.

            She folds up the paper and gives to him. He kisses it.

JACK   Until tonight!

            She kisses him goodbye, then as she leaves, she crosses with JENNY HOOD *and* FREDDIE PERIPHERAL, *who enter.*

HANNAH   Ta-ta!

            She goes.

JACK   Well? What make you of my latest doxy?!

FREDDIE   I thought I recognised her.

JENNY   Too posh.

JACK   Jenny Hood, you are dull. Only interested in a girl if she passes your rigorous political tests.

JENNY   I'll certainly never do it with a Tory.

JACK   Ah! Principles! Principles are a sham. If I've
            learnt one thing since I came to London it's that
            everyone's out for themselves. All this pretence
            about making things better? It's just cover for
            putting yourself first. Everyone's on the make, so
            until my dying day, I intend to capitalise.

JENNY   What an alteration from the well-meaning boy we
            took in

FREDDIE   But if that's the case, why are you our friend?
            We're poor as.

JACK   Because young Frederick, unlike those out there, at
            least we are brutally honest about who we are.
            Jenny Hood is a thieving anti-capitalist intellectual.
            You, a sex-obsessed workaholic. And as for myself,
            my sole concern is freedom and pleasure in all its
            many forms. A libertine, if you will! Our abode is a
            unique island, of countercultural laissez-faire. 'Tis
            why we attract so many visitors. I'faith, sometimes
            the mornings by our bathroom are like Piccadilly
            Circus. A criss-cross of tantalising strangers. They
            love it, and so do I! Oo.

            He winces slightly. A twinge.

FREDDIE   You okay?

JACK   Just an athletic night! Speaking of which, Fred,
            I'm in need.

FREDDIE   Now?! We've got things to do.

JACK   Yes I need to do something as well, quite
            urgently –

            JACK *kisses* FREDDIE, *as* JENNY *starts to move
            the table to the middle of the room and put chairs
            behind it.*

            Jen – Fred and I might be a moment?

FREDDIE   We've got people coming.

JACK   I'll have *people coming* in about / ten minutes if
            you –

FREDDIE   It's important.

JACK   (*Pointing to himself.*) Freddie, it's first thing in the
            morning! We are talking stick of fucking rock.

FREDDIE   Look I'll suck you off later if you concentrate.

JACK   On what?

FREDDIE   It's in the house diary.

JACK   What house diary?

FREDDIE   On the side.

JACK   What side?

FREDDIE   Do you never listen?

JACK   Just staring into those eyes…

FREDDIE   You prefer that girl.

JACK   Oh well yes I can't deny it.

FREDDIE   I thought I – Hannah Tweetwell! That's her! She's
            well known in London PR circles as the ultimate
            social media consultant. Never tweets a thing
            herself, but knows all the scandal, all the strings.
            Advises everyone of import. And she was here!

JACK   Indeed, in our very house. And what's wrong with
            scandal? Isn't that the very apex of life, to test its
            limits? To, with impulse and pleasure, create the
            very heavens here on earth

FREDDIE   She might get someone to tweet about you.

JENNY   I doubt it.

JACK   Why not! I'm pretty scandalous aren't I?

JENNY   You're debauched Jack but not scandalous
            because you have absolutely no shame.

            JACK opens a bottle of wine.

You stride through life believing you can somehow avoid consequence.

JACK   Indeed. Life is short. I leave consequence to others!

JACK is about to drink the wine, but has another twinge…

Ow!

JENNY   Speaking of short, our list of three this morning has shrunk to one. His name is 'Steven'. An IT consultant from the north.

JACK   The north?! Oh!

JENNY   – I know and look, we don't have to go with him, but every week we have an empty room none of us can afford, we've rejected twenty-two people already –

FREDDIE   That's mostly Jack's doing –

JENNY   I augment our fairly earned cash best as I can but if we keep going, we'll run out, at which point we lose the flat. And as we are all without parents or back-up, that means at best a charitable sofa and at worst, the hardened street itself.

The buzzer goes. FREDDIE goes to the intercom and presses a button.

Jack put something on.

JACK   Why?

JENNY   You're bulging unhelpfully.

JACK   Hmm? Ah yes.

He goes. A moment. Then there's a knock at the door.

FREDDIE goes to open it.

FREDDIE   Come in.

He stands out the way, and PHOEBE enters, dressed as 'Steven'.

JENNY   Morning! I'm Jenny Hood. This is –

FREDDIE   Frederick Peripheral at your service. You must be
            Steven.

PHOEBE   Er. Yeah.

FREDDIE   Steven what?

PHOEBE   Steven... er... Man.

JENNY   (*Suspicious.*) Steven Man?

FREDDIE   And what brings you to London?

PHOEBE   Er... Only gone and got a job as an IT consultant
            mate.

            *They both take a moment to appreciate this
            slightly weird turn of phrase.*

FREDDIE   Hmm, well that sounds totally enthralling. If you
            take a moment, we're just awaiting our third.

PHOEBE   No problem.

            (*Aside.*) What hellhole is this? The very walls are
            debauched, and the floor sticks with immoral goo!

            JACK *enters, wearing a gown. He heads straight
            for the wine.*

JACK   The best of mornings to you stranger, applicant
            unto our Utopia! Thou, deemest Steven, what
            makes you believe you have the sheer bloody vim
            to enter us so boldly? – Oh.

            He finally looks at 'Steven'. PHOEBE *is
            uncomfortable.*

PHOEBE   What? Is there a problem mate?

JACK   No I... it's peculiar but you're... Have we met
            before?

PHOEBE   Don't think so.

JACK   They said you were from the north. I too, many
            eons ago, hail from those blust'ry monochrome

lands. But no matter, some refreshment! I performed a single day of service at Pizza Express (never again, let me tell you) and was quickly dismissed for over-serving. However, as I was instructed to the door, I liberated my own severance pay, the alcoholic libation you see before you.

PHOEBE   (*Aside*.) Can this appalling kleptomaniac truly be my angel brother?

Wine? But... it's so early?

JACK   Indeed! Lubricate the diem. Now I'm going to ask you some very personal questions if that's alright, *Steven*? Because if we're going to live together, there'll be no hiding. Betwixt these thinnest of walls, defecation, fornication, and masturbation are all public activities. We will hear you and you, my boy, will hear *us*, doing all of those things, possibly simultaneously. You'll have no need of privacy – whatever your guilty secret – pornography, Starbucks, Sunday Times Culture section, come out! Proud! No judgement! We don't want to lie to each other, or ourselves. No dissembling Steven!

PHOEBE   (*Aside*.) No dissembling?! Better my virtuous lie than his vile truth

JACK   So tell us. What are you? Single, married, divorced? Celibate, total slut?

PHOEBE   Oh. Wot? Me mate? Well I'm a straight man, as you can see, so I like football, and cars, growing chillis, barbecues, and stag dos, beer and locker rooms not reading books stubble mate yeah Jordan Peterson podcasts boxing horror four-hour body can't say it these days mate but legs and pussy can't say anything these days mate yeah gambling other men mostly ego shouting in groups of lots of men sport just men you know normal. Normal. Normal men things. Sport. Yeah mate.

Another moment where all that lands. JACK
unsure…

JACK   Hmm.

PHOEBE   But you? What do you all do for a living?

JENNY   Well although I'm ferociously anti-capitalist, and
            steal from the rich as often as I can, as a
            transitional strategy I also work part-time in a
            café. Jack's… between employment… and Fred…
            well, he – you know I've never understood exactly
            what it is he –

FREDDIE   Oh I could enlighten you, if you want? It's
            actually tremendously interesting, essentially I –

JACK   Steven thank you so much for travelling to see us
            but I do believe –

JENNY   That you would be a welcome addition to our
            home, yes Freddie?

JACK   Peripheral…

FREDDIE   I… er… like you very much.

JENNY   (*Knowing.*) Yes. Good. And I like you too. So just
            one approval left. What do you think Jack? Would
            Steven be a good support to keep this roof above
            our heads?

            JACK *inspects 'Steven'.*

JACK   Steven I have no choice, you may reside, if you
            desire?

PHOEBE   Oh thanks mate, I do.

FREDDIE   Excellent. All agreed!

JACK   It seems so, but in happier news, tonight heralds
            the most prestigious event in town! Hannah
            Tweetwell has requested my presence and we
            must attend.

            He produces the piece of paper and gives it to
            JENNY. *She reads.*

You'll gain us entry Jenny, won't you? Utilise your powers for three golden tickets.

JENNY   Not three Jack, four.

JACK   What? Oh. Really?

FREDDIE   Of course. Steven, would you like to come?

PHOEBE   Where?

JENNY gives PHOEBE *the piece of paper. She reads:*

The Netflix Masked Ball.

She gasps.

(*Aside.*) I can think of nothing worse, and yet this may be my chance to see his full depravity.

(*To the group.*) Indeed it sounds a right laugh mate. I'll happily come.

JENNY   Then a toast!

They pick up their wine glasses. PHOEBE *reluctantly does the same.*

In pursuit of Jack's maiden, in pursuit of pure fun.

We'll venture to town, and Steven, shall come!

They laugh and drink. JACK *looks suspiciously at 'Steven'.*

ACT TWO

Scene One

Lady Susan Climber's house. Hampstead.

LADY SUSAN CLIMBER *sits, flipping through pictures on an iPad.* CARSON, *her doddery manservant, hovers, waiting –*

LADY C.   Too crass. Too poor.

Yuck.

Carson, once again your capacity for failure astounds. All I ask for is some well-bred, rich, gullible and not-entirely unattractive target for my attentions, yet your suggestions are either impoverished cretins or monstrous blobs.

CARSON   I'm sorry madam I did my best, let me try again –

LADY C.   Stop talking. You're talking, and it brings me out in hives.

The doorbell rings. CARSON *doesn't move. Then –*

Well?

CARSON   Oh. Excuse me ma'am.

CARSON slowly dodders out. LADY CLIMBER *rolls her eyes.*

LADY C.   That doddering fool! He better not start weeping again. I've made it perfectly clear – Every lachrymose drop that descends from those cataract eyes is docked pro rata.

CARSON enters.

CARSON   Hannah Tweetwell, madam.

LADY C.   At last. Grant her entrance then leave us Carson, and listen not!

CARSON *opens the door and* HANNAH *enters.*
CARSON *leaves.*

HANNAH   Greetings Lady Climber, on this fine morning.

LADY C.   Ms Tweetwell, how effortless you appear with your fashion. It makes quite a change to see / someone who –

HANNAH   An immediate comment on my appearance.

LADY C.   A compliment my dear.

HANNAH   Would you have made it had I been a man?

LADY C.   In my experience men are rarely well dressed, and so hardly ever deserving of such remarks.

HANNAH   You believe men are less well dressed?

LADY C.   Well…

HANNAH   You have just offended all women, and one sentence later, all men. As a candidate for your social media consultant may I offer some advice? Avoid generalisations until you know how to use them.

LADY C.   Oh and what a shame! 'Tis my fault. I should have known, given your youth, two words of conversation and you're *offended*! You could do with… what's the word your generation's always droning on about? Resilience. Which I have in fucking buckets, by the way.

HANNAH   No Lady / Climber –

LADY C.   Born in the poorest circumstances, I was given no favours, I came to town and simply *worked*. Third place on The Apprentice 2015. Now a lifestyle business, a celebrity. All going swimmingly until… well… a tiniest accident on social media and I'm laid low, my custom gone, management turned tail, and hanging to the London scene by a thread. But I will rise again Ms Tweetwell, which is why you're here. I had hoped you might assist me to no longer be simply Lady Susan Climber, but *Dame* Susan Climber, respected by the wealthy, invited to Number 10 receptions, Netflix deals, government procurement, Strictly.

HANNAH   If I may, Lady Climber –

LADY C.   Oh ho! Yes! The snowflake flurries! You'd have me apologise I expect. 'I understand the harm caused by the microaggression of using the disgusting word "Lady" and fully' –

HANNAH   Madam you misunderstand, you can be divisive by all means –

LADY C.   But not *offensive*.

HANNAH   Offence is essential, but Lady Climber, it must be *targeted*.

LADY C.   …Targeted?

HANNAH   My my. We are a beginner. This explains a lot of your recent disasters.

LADY C.   Don't you bloody well / patronise me –

HANNAH   How to explain? Online, one should have a singular focus. You must climb the ladder of *influence*.

LADY C.   I know fully well how to – I beg your pardon? Influence?

            (*Aside.*) I thought her a typical flimsy, but what's this? Grit?

HANNAH   To achieve the maximum cultural influence possible, you have two options. Either will work, but they must be committed to completely. No half measures.

LADY C.   Indeed?

HANNAH   Either you head fully to the right, becry the culture wars, defend tradition, trash progress, and advocate preserving any and all institutions regardless of history or utility.

LADY C.   Or?

HANNAH   Or head fully to the *left*, becry the culture wars,
            trash tradition, *defend* progress, and advocate
            eradicating any and all institutions regardless of
            history or utility. Either will attract thousands of
            idiots, or as we like to call them, *followers*, who
            like things made simple and have no inclination to
            think for themselves. Over this herd you have
            influence. And your goal is achieved.

LADY C.   But what I genuinely believe...?

HANNAH   Is irrelevant. Your choice as to left or right is
            dictated by what you wish to *do* with your
            influence in the real world.

LADY C.   Well I desire reputation and wealth.

HANNAH   And that ambition is achievable, but I believe
            currently you are too timid.

LADY C.   *Timid?!* I know what *you* want, you quivering
            millennial quim. That I should use every platform
            to declare constant virtue? Urgh! Never!

HANNAH   Lady Climber no. Given your... bearing, I would
            venture the left is not for you. Apart from anything
            else, it is a lot of work. One has to keep track daily
            of the latest terms, the relative status of
            movements, interests, et cetera. On the right you
            don't have to worry about any of that! As Mr
            Friedman did espouse, monetary gain is a virtue in
            itself. And the best aspect? Having no principles
            means without a petard, you can never be hoisted.

LADY C.   Uh no no – I'm sorry, you used too many words
            and I lost interest – oh it's so complicated –

HANNAH   Then as a native in a digital world in which you
            are but a tourist, let me be your guide. I believe, if
            you want to succeed, you must be a taboo-
            breaking vox populi, speaking politically
            incorrect, extreme, juicy, irresistible opinions.
            People will take notice, and then, my lady, you
            will really *rise*.

LADY C.   Hmm. Let me pause, walk away, and consider for
           a moment.

           *She walks away to consider for a moment. As she
           does –*

HANNAH   (*Aside.*) Ha! The vanity and arrogance. So keen to
           rise! She doesn't recognise me. Of course not!
           Well good. For it means my revenge will be a
           soup served even colder. I'll build her up higher
           than before, just to see her tumble down hard,
           further, and this time, forever.

LADY C.   So what would you have me do?

HANNAH   Tonight I have secured you an invitation to the
           Netflix Masked Ball.

LADY C.   The event of the season.

HANNAH   Indeed. I will also be in attendance and guide you
           throughout. This –

           She emails a file to LADY CLIMBER*'s iPad,
           which she picks up and looks at.*

           – would be your costume. Further, I would ask
           that you trust me with your social media. I will
           send a number of tweets this afternoon, to
           announce your attendance, and to proclaim your
           new, most unabashed persona. If you are willing
           to proceed?

LADY C.   You seem to be more than the vegan waif I took
           you for. Very well. Consider yourself employed.

HANNAH   Excellent. Convey your passwords. I shall attend
           to everything.

           Oh, I bring one more surprise for you madam, to
           demonstrate my prowess a little further.

LADY C.   I loathe surprises.

HANNAH   This one you may appreciate. It will help your
           ambitions to root yourself firmly in the bed of the
           establishment.

LADY C.   Ms Tweetwell I had the very same idea!

HANNAH   To this end I believe tonight is an opportunity for you to be accompanied by a gentleman of interest.

LADY C.   We are of one mind. Excellent. But who?

HANNAH   I have taken the liberty to arrange a meeting between yourself, and one of our most distinguished yet susceptible MPs –

LADY C.   Who?! Damn your eyes!

HANNAH   Matt Eton MP.

LADY C.   Matt Eton MP!

She thinks. Then brings him up on her iPad.

Matt Eton MP... Let me look on him. Well his gait is most fine, emanating power with every step, and that hair! Receeding so elegantly from his smooth and pasty brow. His breeding's impeccable, his wallet vast in girth and 'tis undeniable his varied interests sprawl across our well-oiled city... Ms Tweetwell? 'Tis an excellent choice.

HANNAH   That pleases me, for I have asked him to call on you.

LADY C.   When?

A doorbell. LADY CLIMBER *gasps.*

HANNAH   I shall withdraw, and leave you to make the invitation in the flesh.

LADY C.   My gratitude Ms Tweetwell!

HANNAH *goes.*

(*Aside.*) Well! After so long, from my lowly beginnings I feel this is the moment. I must be magnificent, and put to use my skills in dealing with the noble elite. For this man is at the very heart of the establishment, rising fast, privately educated, and refined to boot.

CARSON *re-enters.*

CARSON   The Secretary of State for Procurement, Lady
          Climber.

          MATT ETON *enters*.

LADY C.   Matthew Eton! As I live and breathe.

MATT   Yes, and the fact you still do is entirely down to
          me Lady Climber, for it was my tremendous
          leadership that saw us through the plague.

LADY C.   I know that well. You were a literal *inspiration*.

MATT   I'm afraid I can't stay long. I'm on my way to the
          tailor's for a new suit. The seat is near worn
          through. I'm a keen rider you know.

LADY C.   I'm sure.

MATT   But when I received your invitation I knew I had
          to make a detour.

          I have it that your conversation can be very
          stimulating.

LADY C.   Well indeed, for stimulation is often required.

MATT   Really? Mmm.

          Beat.

LADY C.   How's your wife Mr Eton?

MATT   My wife? Oh, a journalist for the Daily Mail.
          Lifestyle, culture. She pokes the woke. Nothing of
          consequence.

LADY C.   But how does she fare?

MATT   Well she's – yes. You know. Home. The children.
          That sort of thing.

LADY C.   And how *are* the children?

MATT   Ah – young. And there's a lot of them. Four. But
          as a devoted family man I have a rule! I'm there,
          every night, at bathtime. You know I'm very busy
          and I have an extremely important job, but despite

that, every evening I make sure I'm home, I roll my sleeves up, and I *run* those taps, and, I'm *there*, so as the nanny bathes the children they can see their father's face, just... behind her.

LADY C.   May I make a confession?

MATT   Please do.

LADY C.   I can't stand children.

MATT   What a shame. Never wanted them?

LADY C.   They suck the pleasure from your life.

MATT   Oh, well, that's a –

He looks around to check no one's listening, then –

I feel the same! It's true they're awful, but you can't say that, can you?

LADY C.   You can say anything to me.

MATT   I've known my wife since Oxford, but she's become a tyrant, insisting I do this, don't do that. I work just to get away from her, but then in the evenings she forces me home because there's 'things to discuss' or because she's out and apparently it can't be the nanny 'all the time'. So I must confess, in frustration, I crave to venture down other avenues.

LADY C.   Which avenues?

MATT   New frontiers. Mountains. Beautiful valleys and towering... towers. Could be men, women, I wouldn't mind as long as they were *new*. And what would be the harm eh? So long as she doesn't find out.

LADY C.   Mr Eton I have a dilemma.

MATT   Really? Well I am known as a fixer in the party, excellent at resolving dilemmas – Pray continue.

LADY C.   Tonight I am due to attend the Netflix Masked Ball
           in Central London. It's a very exclusive event.
           Celebrities, media types, the great and the good.

MATT   It sounds a most wonderful affair.

LADY C.   I am sure it will be, for Netflix has a lot of money.

MATT   Everyone likes Netflix don't they? I adore Selling
           Sunset. I watch it and imagine I was living that
           life, and not my own.

LADY C.   Hmm. Well tonight, at the party, I would very
           much like to be accompanied. For as a woman,
           you know I am naturally shy and dainty, in need of
           masculine protection.

MATT   I am a man.

LADY C.   Yes and I had some idea – it seems ridiculous now
           – but I had thought I may ask you –

MATT   I see…

LADY C.   But you've said of course you must be home with
           your family in the evening, so I wondered –

MATT   Well hold on –

LADY C.   – is there anyone else you can think of who might
           be appropriate?

MATT   – When I said –

LADY C.   Your counterpart in the opposition perhaps? He
           always seems like an agreeable sort –

MATT   Lady Climber! I would be most happy to
           accompany you!

LADY C.   You would? But what of your wife?

MATT   I loathe her.

LADY C.   Or your children?

MATT   Despise them all.

LADY C.   Well that's wonderful!

MATT   Of course I must continue to be seen as a faithful
            husband, and devoted father, or my career in
            Conservative politics will be... more difficult.
            Therefore, shall we say that you and I are old
            friends? And ideally you would be... perhaps...
            in mourning, so I could be supporting you
            emotionally. How are your parents?

LADY C.   Long departed I'm afraid.

MATT   What about siblings?

LADY C.   I have no family at all.

MATT   Does anyone know that?

LADY C.   I... No, I don't think so –

MATT   Excellent, then your sister Doris recently passed
            away in a terrible accident. After a period of
            seclusion, you are now keen to pay tribute to her
            by re-entering public life. I am your longstanding
            rock, encouraging you to carry on, as she would
            have wanted.

LADY C.   My lord, what a web of lies you create! With such
            ease!

MATT   As a Secretary of State it's practically second
            nature. Now I must needs be tailored, the jodhpurs
            can wait. You said a masked ball. So I will know
            you, pray tell me your costume.

LADY C.   I will be...

            She looks at the iPad again.

            ...a ninja. Think Black Widow.

MATT   Gosh. A strong female protagonist. Just the ticket.
            What time does it begin?

LADY C.   Seven.

MATT   An excellent number! No bathtime for me. I will
            see you there. Farewell Lady Climber!

LADY C.   Goodbye sir, until this evening.

He exits.

Well!

My evening's transformed! Let the games begin!

And with such a fine hand I will play, to win...

ACT THREE

Scene One

The Netflix Masked Ball, Central London.

Music, guests. Champagne and canapés.

Enter JENNY *and* FREDDIE *dressed as waiters, serving the guests.* JENNY *looks around then gestures offstage.*

Enter JACK *and* PHOEBE, *both dressed for the party, masked, in costume.* JENNY *gives them a lanyard.* JACK *is dressed as a lion.* PHOEBE, *as 'Steven', is dressed as a knight.*

JENNY   Here you go. Me and Fred'll get changed into costume later, once we clock off.

PHOEBE   No problem.

JACK   I don't see why you have to work.

JENNY   Opportunity, young Jack!

FREDDIE   And we need the rent. See you later!

            FREDDIE *and* JENNY *pick up trays.* FREDDIE *goes off.* JACK*'s awkwardly with* PHOEBE. PHOEBE *is looking round.*

JACK   Steven, I must leave you, for Hannah Tweetwell is out there somewhere, and I must accost!

PHOEBE   Well good, then I will go with you, and be your wingman mate. Right?

JACK   Right...

            JACK *and* PHOEBE *move off, as* SIR DENNIS HEDGE *enters and moves centre.* JENNY *approaches with her tray, eyeing up his watch...*

JENNY   Canapé sir?

SIR D.   Oh thank you.

JENNY   Wait! You're Sir Dennis Hodge.

SIR D.   Hedge.

JENNY   One of those dinosaurs.

SIR D.   Dragons.

JENNY   You invest in things. But haven't you long since left that most capitalist display, rejecting celebrity? So what are you doing here?

SIR D.   I am asking the same question, young lady, but well... from the poorest start in South London, my inventions have made me somehow unbelievably rich. However now, with advancing years, I ponder my purpose on this earth. I'm keen to invest not simply for profit, but in people. Schemes that might make the world *better*. I was told there might be individuals like that here. Creatives. Young visionaries. But so far... nothing.

JENNY   You could give the cash to me.

SIR D.   But why? Do you have some way to improve the world?

JENNY   Actually I'd probably burn it. I think money is the cause of most of our problems.

SIR D.   Ah! There you are! Half of you are deluded utopian dreamers like yourself and those that aren't seem wholly absorbed with their appearance, status and 'career'. Where's the vision? The gleaming future? Never mind. Thank you for this, at least young lady...

JENNY   May I shake you by the hand sir. Despite your rampant capitalism, I'm a big fan.

SIR D.   Oh very well.

They shake hands. Then SIR DENNIS *moves off.* JENNY *holds up his watch, which she's stolen, then pockets it and moves away as as* HANNAH

enters, on her phone. JACK *and* PHOEBE
reappear and watch her from the side.

JACK   Oh Steven! Have I yet regaled you with what she
            can do with her toes?

PHOEBE   Yeah, many times. It's like you only think about sex.

JACK   Why no! Of a day I contemplate other stimulants.
            Drinking, drugs and gambling are held in equal
            esteem, but now, in this moment I have no need of
            them, for there she is – a fix, a risk and a
            quenching gulp, all in one. Steven when I
            approach, make sure you convey all the many
            wondrous things about me.

PHOEBE   I hardly know you.

JACK   Then improvise!

            He goes across to her. PHOEBE *follows
            reluctantly.*

HANNAH   Jack! You made it past security.

JACK   As I inevitably would. No burly guard or petty
            guest list would restrain my attendance to your
            company.

HANNAH   You're certainly keen, I'll say that.

JACK   Not keen. That reeks of sordid desperation. I'm
            passionate! For I say without a hollow boast, that
            I could have a night with any floozy here that took
            my taste.

HANNAH   Quite a claim.

JACK   My young friend will confirm. Fair Steven, am
            I not held in awe by all and sundry for my
            attractive look and sexual charm?

PHOEBE   (*Aside.*) What should I say? I'll not assist his
            deception of this demure young woman.

            Nah mate, load of bullshit. He's chatting you up
            love.

JACK   You... what?

PHOEBE   Just an average guy with a big mouth.

HANNAH   Ha! You're sure this is your friend? He pulls you down to earth most roughly.

JACK   He's joking i'faith! Such a laughable idea. So, shall we have a drink?

            Enter LADY CLIMBER (*dressed as trouser-suit ninja*).

HANNAH   Hmm. Not now.

            She goes across to LADY CLIMBER. JACK, *rejected, leaves, pursued by* PHOEBE.

LADY C.   Tweetwell! A magical witch! For ever since the errant Instagram, my presence has generated not tremulous excitement but awkward silence. Tonight however, the weather's changed. All do seek my audience!

HANNAH   Indeed Lady Climber, all here pay close attention to where the hottest air blows. Now be sure to stay on the side of outrage. Take every opportunity in conversation to provoke and cause controversy.

            PETER MEDIA OBE *and* ROSALIND DOUBLE-BUDGET *come across.* HANNAH *accosts them.*

            Lady Climber, may I introduce Rosalind Double-Budget?

ROSALIND   Dooble-Booshay. I have my own production company.

HANNAH   And Peter Media OBE.

PETER   Lady Climber, a pleasure.

LADY C.   Well fuck you both.

            A brief moment. Then PETER *and* ROSALIND *burst into laughter.*

PETER   Wonderful!

ROSALIND Hilarious! Lady Climber, I earlier read your witty and provocative tweets about immigration.

LADY C.   Immigration?

ROSALIND Most honest. You dare to say what we're all thinking!

LADY C.   Good! Yes! And wait for more, for I have much to add about... um...

HANNAH   (*Whispers*.) Self-censorship

LADY C.   Self-censorship. And er...

HANNAH   (*Whispers*.) Will Smith.

LADY C.   Will Smith.

ROSALIND I cannot wait! And you've quite a platform yourself, I note your followers grow exponentially. I wondered if you'd thought about television? Hosting a talk show perhaps? Or something at breakfast on ITV?

          TOM DOUBLE-BUDGET *enters, dressed in casual clothes, and with a canvas man bag*.

          Oh excuse me – My son! Can't you see the style? Where's your costume?

TOM   In the bag.

ROSALIND But why not on your person? I pulled every string to get you access to this event, and this is how you repay me, dressed as a layabout.

TOM   Oh... / Mum...

ROSALIND You say you want to work in the media –

TOM   Not the / media, film –

ROSALIND – but how do you intend to do that when your actual mother gives you an opportunity anyone would die for and you throw it in her face?!

TOM   I just don't think networking is how I'm going to make an impact.

PETER *laughs.*

Who is he?

PETER   What kind of film, young man?

TOM   I want to create documentaries about the world,
            collaborate with interesting people, make a
            difference.

ROSALIND I'm sure you do, but who's going to pay for them?

TOM   None of my heroes dress up or do things like that...

PETER   And who, may I ask, are your heroes?

ROSALIND He adores Ken Loach.

PETER   (*Sniggers.*) Oh my god! Really? If that's your
            plan, I'd get your costume on and get out there
            pronto young man!

ROSALIND Or go home.

            He looks at her.

TOM   Fine.

            He goes off. ROSALIND *turns back to* PETER,
            HANNAH *and* LADY CLIMBER.

ROSALIND Twenty-two and still untouched...

PETER   Unsurprising.

ROSALIND But you know, as his mother, I don't mind that at
            all. For despite everything I love him dearly, and I
            honestly dread him growing up and leaving home.
            Therefore if someone were to so much as graze his
            precious innocence... well... I don't know what
            I'd do. But it would probably involve legal action.

            Anyway. Exciting! I will be in touch tomorrow. I
            can see it now!

            'Lady Climber Meets...'

            Let's make this show!

            PETER *and* ROSALIND *move away.*

LADY C.   A show of my own! Tweetwell, your plan bears
           fruit!

HANNAH   Indeed.

           (*Aside*.) And how that fruit will rot!

           HANNAH *moves away.* SIR DENNIS *enters, and*
           nearly bumps into LADY CLIMBER.

SIR D.   Oh I do apologise – Lady...

           He looks up. And immediately they both take a
           step back.

           ... Climber!

LADY C.   Sir Dennis. I had no idea you would be in
           attendance.

SIR D.   If I had known of *your* invitation, believe me I
           would have attended elsewhere. Your messages
           today have been most repulsive. 'Twas hard to
           believe they came from your own hand. I was...
           disappointed.

           He walks on.

LADY C.   (*Aside*.) Oh! I wish he had not read those tweets.
           But why do I care?

           MATT, *dressed in a Harlequin costume, enters,*
           and looks around the room. He takes down his
           mask to look, and LADY CLIMBER *sees him.*

           But here! The game begins!

           LADY CLIMBER *puts her own mask on.* MATT
           spies her, restores his mask, and comes over.

MATT   A ninja with quite a pose!

LADY C.   I thank you. What am I to make of this costume?
           That my mystery man is mischievous?

MATT   I know not what the costume means. I studied
           PPE at Oxford, not *commedia dell'arte*. But I
           liked the hat.

They begin to move away –

Pray let me enquire, does your dark costume portend some recent loss, perchance?

LADY C.   Sadly yes. My sister Doris. Many have expressed their sympathy this evening.

MATT   Then allow me to extend my own.

LADY C.   All in good time, you cheeky sir!

They go. ROSALIND *and* PETER *turn to* SIR DENNIS. JENNY *appears, eyeing up* ROSALIND*'s jewellery…*

ROSALIND   Sir Dennis! We were conversing 'pon the steps we must make to diversify our industry. A subject that I'm sure will be close to your heart.

SIR D.   Of course but I don't think we need to –

PETER   We consider it an absolute priority. I think we both –

ROSALIND   Yes both!

PETER   We saw the Black Lives Matter movement –

SIR D.   No.

PETER   And absolutely.

ROSALIND   Absolutely!

PETER   *Absolutely* felt the moment had come to *do* something. Our industry is so hideously white, and when I saw what was happening on the street.

SIR D.   You saw it on the street? You mean you went out yourself and –

PETER   No – God no, on the TV, obviously —

ROSALIND   I took the knee right where I was watching it, right by my pool house. The cleaner, she was very impressed, I told her: quickly! Take a picture – for my knees aren't what they were – and eventually she managed it, stupid woman, and I put it on my Instagram in total solidarity.

SIR D.   Forgive me, how long have you both been
             working in television?

PETER   Ooooh twenty-five –

ROSALIND Thirty –

PETER   Yes thirty years. We met when we were young.
             Cambridge!

ROSALIND Cambridge I'm afraid! Footlights!

PETER   Footlights!

SIR D.   Thirty years?

PETER   Indeed yes, on and off.

SIR D.   Yet you only thought it was time to do something
             last year?

PETER   Well, yes. I mean that's when it all started wasn't it?

SIR D.   Excuse me, I must be elsewhere.

ROSALIND But sir we've so much to ask you about your
             wealth of experience.

PETER   And more importantly your experience of wealth.

SIR D.   (*Moving on.*) No. No, I'll never work with people
             like you. You're arrogant, lazy, entitled and
             unbelievably racist.

PETER   Oh I know! We are! So massively racist!

JENNY   Drink, sir?

SIR D.   Thank you.

             PETER *and* ROSALIND *move off. As they do,*
             PHOEBE *and* JACK *enter.*

             JACK *is drinking.*

JACK   Some wingman you are! Every time I reach for a
             drink you knock it over, and when I approach any
             saucy you point out my faults, and they run a mile!

             They reach SIR DENNIS *and* JENNY…

JENNY   Sir Dennis, let me introduce my friend Jack, and this is… Steven. Sir Dennis was telling me he's seeking an investment opportunity. He wants to give someone lots of money.

JACK   Then sir! Invest in us!

SIR D.   Why?

JACK   Well… because we represent the most wonderful potential! An intense and dynamic vitality, which runs through our veins, soars through our minds, surely any investment you make would repay a thousandfold!

SIR D.   Oh young man, you make me sad. So many words, yet nothing to say, when the world needs such improvement. Ah, it seems tonight is a lost cause, I'm sure one day I'll strike some gold, or at least, some hope.

    He makes to go. JENNY *takes out his watch.*

JENNY   Um… sir…? You… dropped this.

SIR D.   (*Taking it.*) Oh. Well thank you. Thank you!

    He goes, putting it back on. He crosses with FREDDIE, *entering, holding an empty tray.*

    Excuse me.

    FREDDIE *lets him past.* JACK *looks at* JENNY, *surprised.*

FREDDIE   I'll wait no longer! You too Hood. Let's head into the kitchen and re-emerge bedazzled and bejewelled.

JACK   Don't see why you two felt the need to work anyway.

JENNY   Zounds Jack I can't pay for everything with grift!

FREDDIE   To make up for your debt. Why near three months' rent owed –

JACK   We have an arrangement, you need not –

PHOEBE   So Jenny works in her café. And Freddie works –
           actually I never found out what you do –

FREDDIE   Oh well, yes I just –

PHOEBE   (*Ignoring him – back to* JACK.) Surely you could
           seek an occupation?

           JACK *winces slightly. As if in pain.*

           Cos it seems quite unfair to let them do it all.

JACK   (*To* PHOEBE.) You know… You remind me of
           someone.

PHOEBE   Funny. As I feel I don't know you at all. Mate.

           They look at each other. A moment…

JACK   I'll ask that from now sir, you leave me
           thoroughly to myself.

           JACK *goes, grabbing another drink.*

FREDDIE   Come Hood, let's recostume. These two need a
           laugh.

           FREDDIE *goes.* JENNY *about to follow but sees*
           PHOEBE *unhappy.*

JENNY   Try not to worry. 'Tis Jack's way, especially a
           sheet or two to the wind. He'll bounce in the
           morning. 'Tis always the same.

PHOEBE   But how can you live with one who has no morals.
           He talks of freedom, but it's simply an excuse for
           selfishness, is it not? Freddie works. You steal but
           only from the very rich. But how can one bear to
           be around… that!…

JENNY   He has a good heart.

PHOEBE   A good… heart?

JENNY   Yes. One must look behind the surface. Isn't that
           right… Steven?

PHOEBE   I… Well… yes… but –

           JENNY *takes* PHOEBE's *moustache off.*

I... I can explain!

JENNY smiles and goes, leaving PHOEBE on her own.

Formal dancing begins around her, swirling our guests around and causing confusion.

As it does, a HARLEQUIN enters, awkwardly. He's masked and holding two drinks.

PHOEBE sees him looking, before she can put the moustache back on.

The HARLEQUIN offers a drink, and then takes some awkward steps across to give it to PHOEBE.

She smiles and takes it.

The HARLEQUIN takes off the mask. It's TOM. He breathes deeply.

Sir you're in distress! Perhaps you should have chosen a different mask?

TOM   My mother said given my appearance it should cover every last inch.

PHOEBE   Your mother?

TOM   I thought coming here would be good for my career. Not that I have one yet, but I so *desire* to make documentaries! About important subjects and attempt through the power of the screen to change the world.

PHOEBE   That sounds like a noble aim.

TOM   Mum thinks it ridiculous.

PHOEBE   I don't believe it's ridiculous at all.

TOM   You don't?

PHOEBE   Indeed no. For though one may laugh at our dreams, about how we want to change the world, it's through aiming at stars that we may at least achieve the moon.

TOM   Well... yes, I think that's right. But tell me about
             yourself. What brings you here?

PHOEBE   Oh... just to see what it's like, I suppose. To
             discover if I... get on with anyone. But I'm...
             disappointed.

TOM   I get on with so few people.

PHOEBE   The same.

TOM   I hardly ever meet anyone, is the truth. But I often
             imagine there might come a day I do, and we
             just... click.

PHOEBE   Click, indeed.

TOM   I don't mean sex of course, don't for a moment
             think I mean that.

PHOEBE   There's nothing wrong with sex though, is there?

TOM   Oh nothing at all, I mean sex is lovely, probably, I
             don't know, but more important for me is a
             meeting of *minds*.

PHOEBE   Precisely. I mean I have sexual thoughts, I mean I
             have done it, I'm very sex positive, but when I've
             actually had intercourse with boys it's... not quite
             lived up to expectations...

TOM   Maybe it's not the right person...

PHOEBE   Yes! You know I think it might be because the
             feeling wasn't there, you know – the true, higher,
             pure...

TOM *and* PHOEBE   *...connection*

             They gasp, then stare at each other, amazed.

TOM   Would you care to dance?

PHOEBE   Why yes...

             ROSALIND *appears and goes over to* TOM.

ROSALIND Tom what are you doing? Who's this?

TOM   She's... er... sorry I didn't get your name.

PHOEBE   Phoebe.

ROSALIND What does she do?

TOM   I... don't know.

ROSALIND A waste of time! I've told you. Network!

                She takes him away.

                PHOEBE *stands, sadly watching him go offstage.*

                As she does, from out of the dance, another
                HARLEQUIN *appears.*

                PHOEBE *turns and faces them. Confused for a*
                moment.

HARLEQUIN   What do you think?!

PHOEBE   You... but you were just –

                The HARLEQUIN *takes her head off. It's* JENNY.

                Oh!... there's another Harlequin.

JENNY   I'm not surprised. There was an offer in the hire
                shop.

PHOEBE   You should ensure there's no confusion. I'm
                sorry –

                She puts her moustache back on.

                I should explain my deception, but please, don't
                tell anyone, certainly not Jack.

JENNY   Why not?

                Enter FREDDIE, *dressed as a ninja – identical to*
                LADY CLIMBER.

FREDDIE   Hello! You approve?

PHOEBE   Yes, very nice.

FREDDIE   You think Jack will?

JENNY   Come, let's find him!

They head off. From the side of stage enters…
DEATH, *with a scythe in a bony hand. She crosses, heading after the group.*

As DEATH *goes,* JACK *appears opposite. His shirt is now undone, and he holds a bottle of wine that he's drinking from. He's quite drunk, and is looking for* HANNAH *in the dance.*

JACK   Oh God! Where's Tweetwell? The truth is, despite my protestations, I *am* desperate, for the more I drink the more this sickness grows, and I need *distraction*. Passion. Without it, another night is wasted completely. Life ticking away.

            HANNAH *enters.*

HANNAH   Jack you look undone!

JACK   At last! Ms Tweetwell. I was… concerned I might not discover you again. But here you are. Shall we dance? Please…

            She takes his hand and they go into the dance. The music builds and all dance now: ROSALIND, PETER, TOM, SIR DENNIS, LADY CLIMBER, MATT, FREDDIE, JENNY *and* PHOEBE. *Others in the crowd.*

            LADY CLIMBER *and* SIR DENNIS *come face to face for a moment – shooting daggers – then move apart again.*

            Then JACK *trips and staggers back.* HANNAH *takes a step back too.*

            He recovers and tries to dance with her again –

HANNAH   Jack… what ails you?

            She takes the glass off him.

            I think perhaps… enough.

JACK   What?! No I…

HANNAH   Yes.

JACK   Ah. Of course! So the brakes are slammed. Not by
the police or government. But by each other. For
propriety. Well... *No.*

*He reaches into a pocket in his costume we didn't
know he had and produces a packet of cigarettes
and a lighter. Everyone around slowly stops
dancing and looks at him.*

My pleasure shall not be contained!

He lights a cigarette.

A mild gasp from the crowd.

PHOEBE   Jack!

JACK   Oh this? We should all be able to do it. To drink
what we want, smoke what we like. It used to be
one was free to decide how to spend your time
upon this earth, for better or ill, who you were,
smoker or no-smoker, believer or non-believer,
angel or dirty fucking *devil*, but now you're all...
all of you... the same, really, or not *really*,
because in fact the more you *contain* yourselves,
the more you have thoughts you never say, doubts,
beliefs you hold in your hearts you'd never let
pass your lips, the more the tyranny of *virtue* takes
over, the more you'll be shamed and guilty and
you'll crumble or the more you'll feel resentment
and hurt and want to *fight!* Well not me! I *refuse.* I
am not for virtue but for freedom, for truth! We're
sick of being guilty. I *ought* to do this, I *should* do
that. When inside us all are desires, sexual,
financial, all kinds of cravings and opinions we're
told to hide.

PHOEBE   Jack please –

JACK   Let's talk about forbidden subjects. Expose our
devils and be proud of what they say. Half of us
gaze upon pornography, how many admit it?
What's in the dark nature of our desire? Maybe
thinking of ourselves as victims all the time isn't –

PHOEBE *steps forward and grabs* JACK*'s arm.*

PHOEBE   Jack! Why are you being so awful! You have no
           morals at all!! To speak like this!

JACK   Because I'm *free* Steven. To *play*, to experiment
           with ideas!

PHOEBE   A lame excuse. I thought you were so much better.
           In your heart.

JACK   Why? You don't know me.

PHOEBE   No.

           She removes the moustache.

           But I hoped I did.

JACK   …Phoebe?!

           Oh!

           He feels a sudden pain. SECURITY *grab him.*

PHOEBE   You're just bad, aren't you? A bad person.

JACK   No! No I'm not!

           SECURITY *escort him out.*

           Phoebe! Please!

           *Music starts again, and the party resumes. The
           others disperse…*

           PHOEBE *makes her way to the front of the stage.*

PHOEBE   (*Aside.*) Alas, this shame! Doesn't he see others
           pay the cost for his so-called freedom! His
           cancerous smoke that none can escape. He may
           find these fascinating ideas to be freely discussed,
           but many, like myself, find them part of a
           dangerous discourse. Note it is often the men who
           crave this kind of freedom! Note it is often the
           drunk and unhappy! This talk of releasing the
           darkness within us comes from older generations
           who with no access to therapy, and a deeply

conservative society, used drugs and drink as
self-medication. In vino non veritas. In vino is just
escape! And all this from him! It makes no sense.
How can he be full of such bile when I am not?!
How can he not see the hurt he causes?! Our
so-called 'rules' he rails against enforce only
kindness, but now I see it is precisely that kindness
he cannot stand. For he is not kind. There is so
much to fight in the world, and he chooses to fight
us. Well then. He is the very devil and he is lost!

A waiter passes with a drink.

I've been on orange for the night. But with my life
in turmoil, perhaps a dose of poison is the cure.
This one time, maybe I will escape myself.

She downs the drink.

Disgusting.

But oh. My head.

*From this moment, the world of the play begins to
collapse – music through to the interval – it
develops a dreamlike quality…*

Waiter!

She takes another, downs it.

The HARLEQUIN *approaches and puts out his
hand.*

That beautiful mask. I know who you are. For we
spoke earlier, my Harlequin.

She takes the HARLEQUIN*'s hand. He twirls her
round, so she's in his arms. She downs his drink,
and they begin to dance… as… another*
HARLEQUIN *enters.*

*He watches her dancing, cavorting with someone
else.*

*Then takes off his mask and comes downstage to
speak to us.*

TOM   (*Aside*.) I've had a terrible time, but stayed hoping
             to see Phoebe once again, she seemed unfrivolous,
             like myself, unafraid of wondrous seriousness. But
             now she dances with another, so once more, I'm
             left behind. No love for me tonight.

             I'll resume the mask, find my mother, and taxi
             back to my lonely tower.

             He puts the mask back on, as LADY CLIMBER
             enters.

LADY C.   Ah ha! My lord of mischief! I lost you in the glory
             of that young man's meltdown. Wasn't it hilarious?!
             But… o-ho! Something in this light does give your
             frame a much more flattering view. You're standing
             more erect. Taller even. Hmm. Perhaps I've drunk
             too much, but you are quite the titan.

             (*Aside*.) It seems I'll get some pleasure from this
             necessary chore.

             He holds her back and goes to take off his mask.

             Er no no! Keep it on. Be not insulted if I say I find
             you even more attractive with your face
             concealed.

             *She holds his hand, expectant. He resists, but then,
             we see him shrug, and they head off together.*

             As they do, FREDDIE *enters downstage, his mask
             off, to talk to us.*

FREDDIE   As my name suggests, I feel I'm a supporting
             character. That despite my own hopes, and fears,
             I'm simply on the edge of others. I have loved
             Jack for a long time. But he doesn't even notice,
             which is probably why I seek out so much
             meaningless sex. But anyway, enough. I must
             move on. I'll go home, then in the morning, wake,
             and carry on with my real calling, my daily
             occupation, which is –

MATT   Aha! Been looking for you, my fighting floozy.

MATT *has entered upstage.* FREDDIE *quickly puts his mask on.*

Don't be coy.

He goes over to FREDDIE*, and takes his hand. Kisses it.*

FREDDIE *curtsies and they go off together.*

Scene Two

A dark and dirty alley outside the back of the party venue.

JACK *is thrown onto the ground by* SECURITY*. He picks himself up.*

JACK   Ow! Ouch.

He recovers his bravado. Stands tall.

Why do I care?! Let them reject me! I shall not be compelled! Damn their principles and their hellish cancellation! To hell with consequence!

He winces. Then recovers.

This feeling. Worse than ever. What is it that afflicts me so?

Thunderclap.

Oh – I'm so cold. I've no idea where I am. And no fare home neither. I had no pocket for my phone.

There's someone there, in the dark. Perhaps I can ask advice.

Hello!

Hello! I wonder if you might know where I am?

DEATH *appears from the shadows.*

But what's this? No! Too soon!

DEATH *reaches out for him.*

No!

Sudden blackout.

Scene Three

Three separate rooms:

LADY CLIMBER*'s bedroom.*

FREDDIE*'s room.*

PHOEBE*'s room.*

LADY CLIMBER *enters with* TOM (*masked*).

LADY C.   My man of mischief, time to be revealed – all but your face remember?

         She starts to take his costume off.

         PHOEBE *and* JENNY (*masked*) *enter.*

PHOEBE   There's something in your gait I find enticing, the way your body fits with mine, relaxes me. We knew there was a pure connection but this feels like much more! Your company is well… most stimulating. Perhaps –

         JENNY *kisses her. It's passionate.*

         Ahem. Well yes, perhaps if we exchange our numbers we could – oh –

         PHOEBE *suddenly kisses* JENNY – *they fall onto the bed.*

         MATT *enters with* FREDDIE (*masked*).

MATT   Right. Shall we?

*They start to take off each other's costumes, but
leave the masks for now.*

Meanwhile LADY CLIMBER *has finished taking
off* TOM's *costume. He stands in his boxers, and
the mask.*

LADY C.   This is most unexpected! To be your age and look
like this – all these muscles pert and proud. I'd
thought we would turn the lights to low, but let us
leave them full, I want to see my feast! Come! To
bed!

*She pushes him into bed, and removes her costume
to join him. Meanwhile* MATT *is still taking off
his costume –*

MATT   Almost there –

PHOEBE *comes up for air from kissing* JENNY.

PHOEBE   My my! For someone who is less experienced,
you seem rather confident. And there's something
happening in my body that –

JENNY *takes off her mask.*

Oh. Right. Wow. This changes things, but equally,
I've wondered for quite some time if I might be
drawn across the aisle so it's not altogether –

JENNY *puts her finger on* PHOEBE's *lips.*

Okay.

JENNY *disappears beneath the covers, as* MATT
finishes taking off FREDDIE's *costume, and they
stand facing each other.*

MATT   The masks?

FREDDIE *nods, then takes off his mask.*

Oh my god.

FREDDIE   What?

He takes off his own mask. FREDDIE *gasps.*

FREDDIE   Shit.

MATT   Matt Eton, Secretary of State for Procurement.

FREDDIE   I want to be sick.

MATT   I'm very sorry for the misunderstanding.

            But well…

FREDDIE   What?

MATT   Seeing as we're here?

            FREDDIE *looks at him.*

FREDDIE   I must move on…

MATT   What?

FREDDIE   I must!

            He kisses MATT *and they fall onto the bed,
            tearing at each other's clothes.*

            They all fuck.

            *The sound builds. Music, pounding, beds creaking.
            The music continues.*

            Until with –

LADY C.   You fucking god!

MATT   Most enjoyable.

PHOEBE   This is the best night of my liiiiife!

            – an enormous orgasm…and…

            Blackout.

            Interval.

ACT FOUR

Scene One

Lady Climber's house. Living room.

She comes in, in a dressing gown, and sits on the chaise longue.

LADY C.   Well! Who would have thought a lump like him
would be so thorough? Every time I deemed him
surely spent, he, like Jesus, rose again. And
although each occasion was most satisfying,
I don't mind admitting I'm exhausted! Of course
my plan is to use his power and influence to my
own ends, but still... after all our passion, I almost
feel some kind of... affection for him. Perhaps he
could stay around. A strange feeling indeed...

The door opens and the HARLEQUIN *comes in,
loosely dressed in his costume again – still with
the mask.*

Good morning sir!

HARLEQUIN   May I take this off now?

LADY C.   What? Oh, if you must.

*She turns away to the drinks cabinet. He starts to
take off the mask.*

Morning pick-me-up? I'm having a toniced gin,
with lime. To celebrate our night's most
debauched endeavours.

He takes off the mask. It's TOM, *of course.*

TOM   Oh yeah, I guess. Why not? Thanks.

She makes them with her back turned.

I... er... really loved that by the way. I'm not very
experienced, you know

LADY C.   Come sir. We know that's not true.

TOM   But I hope it all… worked?

LADY C.   Indeed it did. Most satisfactory.

TOM   Right. Good. Okay. Cool.

LADY C.   It's strange, I find the way you speak in private conversation so at odds to how you sound on television. More casual somehow.

TOM   Television?

LADY C.   Yes.

TOM   Well, I've not made TV yet, but hopefully –

LADY C.   What nonsense! For during the plague I near daily saw your face behind that little podium.

TOM   A… podium?

She turns with the glasses, holding one out, still focused on them for now –

LADY C.   Yes, whenever you appeared to earnestly deliver some awful medical news, I admired you even then. In fact I was wondering if… this morning we might go and –

She finally looks up and sees TOM.

Oh my christ.

She drops the glass. It smashes on the floor.

TOM   Oops.

LADY C.   Who the fuck are you?

TOM   I'm Tom.

LADY C.   *Tom?* Who's Tom?

TOM   We met yesterday, at the –

LADY C.   But you're… How old are you?

TOM   Twenty-two.

LADY C.   You're the Harlequin.

TOM   Cheapest one in the shop. They had a deal.

LADY C.   They had a... *They had a deal?!* You're not
           supposed to be – I mean –

TOM   I had a great night.

LADY C.   You – I'm sure. Sure you did. Did you?

TOM   Yes.

LADY C.   Yes. Well. That explains a lot I suppose but –

TOM   Are you quite alright?

LADY C.   Yes. No. *No!* I'm not. Not alright at all –

TOM   I thought you said the sex was –

LADY C.   The *sex*? Yes the sex was sex I don't give a fuck
           about the *sex* I need my *money*, my position.

TOM   I thought we did rather well on position.

LADY C.   Don't you dare make light of this you spotty...
           intern.

TOM   I'm confused.

LADY C.   *You're* confused?! Look, you're just... you're not –

TOM   Wait, did you think I was someone else?

LADY C.   Oh you're so incredibly hard of understanding. *Yes,
           yes I* thought you were definitely someone else.

TOM   Oh. Wow.

           *As she carries on talking, he goes and gets out his
           phone. He then presses a button and starts filming.
           She turns out, panicking, not seeing any of this.*

LADY C.   And you're – oh my god you're *that* Tom! The
           producer's son! Rebecca Double-Bucket or
           whoever she was – who's going to give me my
           show, and she said if anyone touched her son –

           She turns to find him filming her.

           What are you doing?

TOM   Well I really want to make documentaries and I did this masterclass online about it, and it said if anything happens to you in your life that's in any way remarkable, start filming straight away, get it online, put your work out there, and this –

She takes the phone out of his hands.

LADY C.   No, no.

TOM   I got a few videos last night too. I can't wait to show Mum! Not her little boy any more!

LADY C.   How do you delete this?

TOM   I can tell you're upset, but I promise I'm just... a guy, you met, and yes it was my first time but I understand that doesn't mean I –

LADY C.   First... time? I just took your virginity?! When your mother said 'innocent' I didn't realise she meant –

TOM   Yeah.

Beat.

LADY C.   Brilliant.

TOM   – but we don't really talk about it like 'taking your virginity' any more as it's sort of offensive and possessive? Anyway it was good so, I'm, well I'm having an 'oh what a beautiful morning' moment you know what I mean? The sun is shining the birds are –

LADY C.   Christ – *listen* – you're not to tell a soul about this, ever. It's all, all of this, deeply problematic, to use one of your generation's ridiculous words. I don't want *anyone* discovering what happened last night.

TOM   Thought you said it was good.

LADY C.   Tom. Tom? Is that your...

TOM   Name?

LADY C.   Name. Yes.

TOM   Tom.

LADY C.   *Tom.* It was fine. Knowing what I know now, I'd
           say it wasn't bad at all, for a first attempt. It was
           certainly persistent. But now it's finished, you're
           not a virgin any more which is yay for you but
           now you need to delete the entire night from your
           head, go away, and never speak about it again.
           Think you can manage that? Good. And this…

           *She takes his phone and puts it in her bag. It's a
           canvas bag – very similar to* TOM*'s. Without
           noticing particularly, she puts the bag down next
           to* TOM*'s.*

           …is confiscated. I'll send you a new one
           tomorrow. Best phone in the world. Whatever you
           want. Now run along and play with your TikToks.

TOM   Why are you ashamed? If you enjoyed it and so
           did I then –

LADY C.   Not ashamed. Just keen for lots of lovely
           discretion. Alright with you?

           A moment.

TOM   Yeah.

LADY C.   Great, so can you… get your things together and
           go away now please?

           TOM *goes and gets his belongings together – sort
           of looking at* LADY CLIMBER. *Not noticing, he
           picks up* LADY CLIMBER*'s bag and puts his
           things into it. As he does,* CARSON *enters.*

CARSON   Ms Tweetwell is here madam.

LADY C.   Oh Carson I've told you to *knock.* And for christ's
           sake would it take too much energy to smile
           sometimes you miserable elf. Go on. See if you
           can. Smile.

           He tries.

           Urgh. Second thoughts never do that again.
           Nightmares.

LADY CLIMBER *turns to* TOM.

Anyway as I say thank you so much for seeing me safely home young man, I hope the spare mattress on the floor was alright to sleep on, as you did all night. Ready to go?

TOM *picks up the bag (the wrong one, but we probably won't notice that here).*

TOM   I... er... I had a really good night. I'll remember it forever.

LADY C.   Lovely. Bye then!

He goes. LADY CLIMBER *turns to* CARSON.

Sweet boy. I took pity on him at the party, he walked me home then was so tired by the time we got here I let him sleep. What a child. Aw.

CARSON *notices some stray boxer shorts on the floor. He picks them up.* LADY CLIMBER *snatches them off him.*

You've signed an NDA Carson. Say a word, and I'll send you back to your previous employer.

CARSON   Oh madam! No! Not Miss Dorries! Anyone but her.

LADY C.   Well then. Watch yourself.

HANNAH   (*From offstage.*) Lady Climber?

LADY C.   Go away.

Once CARSON *has gone,* LADY CLIMBER *stuffs the underwear behind a portrait of herself just as* HANNAH *enters, with an iPad under her arm.*

HANNAH   Lady Climber, how are you this morning?

LADY C.   Quite well, thank you.

HANNAH   You enjoyed last night?

LADY C.   On and off.

HANNAH   Well, it certainly enjoyed you! I have compiled a
           portfolio of attention in the press.

           She hands LADY CLIMBER *the iPad.* LADY
           CLIMBER *looks through it.*

LADY C.   My! All so flattering. So many photographs.

HANNAH   And I'm close to finishing your children's book
           deal for Christmas, appearances on some celebrity
           programmes... oh and already I have received the
           paperwork for your television show with Rosalind
           Double-Budget. I assume you will accept?

LADY C.   With pleasure!

HANNAH   I've tried to call her this morning but she's having
           some family issue. Apparently her son disappeared
           last night and she's not happy.

LADY C.   Ah.

HANNAH   Never mind, I'm sure she'll be in touch. How did
           your evening progress with Mr Eton?

LADY C.   Oh enjoyably enough, but sadly he did not
           accompany me home.

HANNAH   He – oh, that *is* sad. For I had selected him with
           care and anticipated you and he would become
           most entwined.

           (*Aside*.) Fie on her! I had intended an illicit liaison
           with this future prime minister, to be revealed at
           the crucial moment, to add to her disgrace.

           (*To* LADY CLIMBER.) No matter! I shall invite
           him instead to your next event. Today Sir Dennis
           Hedge is hosting a young entrepreneur's reception
           at his Kensington house. You have been requested
           to present one of the awards.

LADY C.   Sir Dennis? Are you sure? For we know each
           other of old and our relationship is most warlike.
           Is he aware of my invitation?

HANNAH   He is and wishes now that you may settle things.

LADY C.   But only last night he said he found my recent tweets 'disgusting'?

HANNAH   And this invitation is useful for our purposes. A high-profile event, but this time *exclusive*. Only the richest, and most influential individuals will be in attendance. Royal family, presidents, Gary Lineker.

LADY C.   Yes of course… Well… Sir Dennis…

A moment of thought. Of… longing, perhaps…

His motives are irrelevant. I shall attend.

HANNAH   Good. As before, I've detailed a suggested outfit for the occasion here…

She pings LADY CLIMBER *a picture on her iPad.*

And I would ask just one more thing. That going forward you avoid uncontrolled personal scandal. It would undermine your judgement of others if you were caught in some… unfortunate incident of your own.

LADY C.   Ms Tweetwell, at my age life is very calm. My scandal days are long forgot.

HANNAH notices something sticking out from the back of the portrait. She take it and pulls and it's the boxer shorts.

She looks at LADY CLIMBER.

Ah! My awful servant Carson uses them to dust and has a filthy habit of depositing them in all sorts of absurd places. I'll thrash him later.

She puts them back.

HANNAH   You seem most dissatisfied with your help. And he is rather ancient. Why do you not source a more efficient and economic serf?

LADY C.   Oh how I wish that were possible! But… sadly, 'tis not. I am most stuck with him.

HANNAH   A shame. Well, please follow my instructions to the letter, and very soon, all will be yours.

LADY C.   Indeed I shall. Farewell.

HANNAH goes.

LADY CLIMBER breathes a sigh of relief and sits on the chaise longue.

I must keep control, for if I can then, as she says, I'll have what I so dearly desire. My revolting father, those bullies in the playground, all of them said I'd amount to nothing, but now I'm close to having it all. There's nothing wrong with wanting more, and doing what it takes!

Now let me lay eyes on my instructions...

She look on the iPad.

Hmm. A strange choice indeed. If Tweetwell had not already proved herself astute, I'd find this costume... questionable.

She stands.

But well... I am committed and she has earned my trust.

She is about to go, but stops and thinks again. As she does, CARSON appears, and watches.

Sir Dennis indeed! 'Tis... absurd. Any relationship we had is long past. *All* my relationships are past, thank heavens. 'Tis the very thing which allows me to thrive.

She gets her bag, picks it up and is about to leave –

CARSON   Surely not *all* relationships, my lady?

LADY C.   Yes, every one. I'm going shopping!

She strides away, leaving CARSON onstage.

Scene Two

Jack Virtue's lodgings. Living room. East London.

In the living room there is an armchair, a sofa, a dressing screen, and a cupboard.

PHOEBE *enters, smiling broadly, holding a bottle of wine, which she swigs out of occasionally. She stretches and sits on the sofa. Then picks up a spliff and tries to light it, but can't get the lighter to work.*

PHOEBE   (*Aside.*) I feel reborn! Of course I had often thought of women, but never realised it could result in such unalloyed and sticky joy as this! I'd wanted everything in such straight lines, but now Jenny has relaxed me, in so many ways, and through our intercourse both verbal and sexual, I see many curves and subtle shades. We're human! In the end. All of us. A unique mix, every one.

                   JENNY *enters, and effortlessly lights* PHOEBE's *spliff, which* JENNY *then smokes.*

JENNY   You seem happy.

PHOEBE   Indeed, 'twas one of the best nights of my life! I haven't slept at all, but I don't care! I'm full of possibility! I wish Jack was here. That I could speak to him…

JENNY   I'm sure he'll turn up. But I still don't understand why you went to all this effort. Why didn't you just call him?

PHOEBE   I've tried to call him now, but he doesn't answer. I want to tell him I get that our ethics are conditioned by the situation, and despite disagreeing perhaps we should… spend some time together.

                   Enter FREDDIE *in pyjamas, eating a bowl of cereal.*

FREDDIE   Morning!

He's followed by MATT, *also in pyjamas.*
FREDDIE *sits down.* MATT *goes to join him, then sees the women.*

MATT   Wait!

            He grabs a cushion and covers his face.

FREDDIE   So this is my flatmate Jenny Hood. And this is – er
            – oh

JENNY   Phoebe.

FREDDIE   You've changed?!

PHOEBE   So much.

FREDDIE   Excellent!

MATT   Frederick, I believe I had most clearly explained I
            could not reveal our most pleasurable endeavours
            to the world.

FREDDIE   Them? They have no care! Ladies if anyone
            should ask about my consort here your lips must
            be most superglued.

JENNY   Okay.

PHOEBE   You have my word.

FREDDIE   (*To* MATT.) See? Your secret's safe.

            MATT *cautiously lowers his cushion, then puts his
            hand out.*

MATT   In that case – Matt Eton, Secretary of State for
            Procurement.

PHOEBE   Oh yes! I remember you from the briefings. I
            watched every day.

MATT   Indeed – it was I that steered our national ship
            safely through the stormy viral seas.

PHOEBE   Safely? Er – we had the highest death rate?

MATT   Well I'm not sure international comparisons are –

PHOEBE   And the greatest hit to our economy –

MATT   Indeed these may be the *facts*, but our country
            moveth quickly on! And I think if we just talk
            about other things enough, we might all forget?

JENNY   Freddie, I find this choice of partner... unusual
            for you.

PHOEBE   Sir why are you so keen to hide?

MATT   Ah well, in truth I'm happily married, with four
            young children, and most keen not to upset them, as
            it would take up so much time, but beyond that
            trifling concern I have a political career that will not
            be served by public knowledge of my infidelity.

JENNY   But what if your wife found out?

MATT   Oh then she'd wield her pen like a sword and
            disembowel me across the Mail on Sunday. But
            I'm hoping it's unlikely. Her brain's most dull
            these days, fogged I believe by hot yoga.

JENNY   But you had a good time last night?

MATT   Oh indeed? It was liberating, in so many ways!

JENNY   Good.

MATT   And revealing.

PHOEBE   I bet.

FREDDIE   And now Matt?

MATT   Ah... Yes. And now I must resign.

JENNY   You... what?

            He starts emailing on his phone.

MATT   Sweet youth, you are right to presume there was an
            initial frenzy of sexual endeavour, but Freddie
            made me promise to stay the night, which, as a man
            of my word, I did, and then, during that night, we
            talked, well, *he* talked, and explained, and educated
            me in ways and worlds I had never imagined. I took
            it all in, and this morning, I am reborn.

PHOEBE   Oh really? Excellent.

MATT   As a Socialist! Red as the robin, Left as luggage.

PHOEBE   Wow. Presumably your wife won't approve of
            that.

MATT   Well, no that's true. Right, email composed.

            Gosh that's true about my wife...

            His finger hovers over the button.

            I'll... er... send it later, if that's alright?

FREDDIE   But Matt, you promised.

MATT   I did, and I will, you have my word. Very soon.
            But now, forgive me, for I must shower
            thoroughly, and attempt with hard Labour to
            cleanse this most Tory Trunk.

            MATT *kisses* FREDDIE *and then goes off to the
            bathroom.*

PHOEBE   He's a man divided. I fear not just for his wife and
            children, but himself. You know one cannot live
            for long with such a chasm in your soul.

JENNY   Many have, and lived quite long. It's up to him.

            The doorbell goes.

PHOEBE   Aha! I know who this is.

JENNY   Pray who? It's too early for a visitor.

PHOEBE   In the middle of the night while you were asleep
            I decided I'd enough of the filth, and used an app
            to order forth a cleaner who would come and start
            the purge! Worry not, I have some savings and
            will pay for it myself.

            She presses the buzzer.

            Come up!

JENNY   Haven't I persuaded you there's value in some
            dirt? Not everything needs be clean – as well you
            did affirm last night!

PHOEBE *goes to the door and opens it, in expectation of the cleaner.*

PHOEBE *Some* dirt yes, and my sexuality may now be open, wine is cool, and ethics complicated, but none of that can help the fact this place is a stinking hole. And it will make a nice surprise for Jack when he returns.

(*Aside*.) *If* he returns…

JENNY *stands*.

JENNY Okay. Up to you. But tell them to start in here, I'm going back to bed.

FREDDIE Yeah me too.

PHOEBE Alright, but do not lounge too long, I thought we could go for a morning…

The doors slam – they're both gone.

…walk.

She turns as a woman, about forty, appears at the door. Casually dressed. This is REBECCA DE SOUZA. PHOEBE*'s rather overexcited.*

Ah! Hi! I'm Phoebe. Come in! Very prompt I have to say.

REBECCA Rebecca. You were expecting me?

PHOEBE Oh yes, but I hadn't dreamed you'd come so soon! Now, please don't turn around and walk straight out again, I know we're facing a mountain, but no one's expecting it all to be done today, and I intend to do most of it myself, once I feel slightly less vomitous and drunk than I do at this moment. If you could just see to the key areas, we're talking kitchen, bathroom, you would be saving these guys' lives, is the truth, you *really* would –

REBECCA This is a flat share?

PHOEBE   Indeed, myself and three others, and there's a
           visitor this morning, Freddie's catch from last
           night, he's using the bathroom at the moment, but
           he'll be out shortly and you can get in there and do
           your thing –

REBECCA   My –

PHOEBE   – you haven't brought cleaning equipment oh that
           was an oversight on my part why on earth would I
           assume *that*? Well stay here 'tis not your
           responsibility but mine I'll run to the shop now –

           *She puts on her coat and shoes. Takes a fabric bag
           from her pocket.*

           – perhaps just start with a tidy while I'm out? I
           used to be very much against the idea of domestic
           help but I was persuaded by a wonderful article
           explaining how it created an economy of
           employment and how that employment had vastly
           better conditions than the gig economy for
           instance I certainly don't look down on it you
           want some chocolate I really want some chocolate
           see you in a minute!

           She goes and closes the front door after her.

REBECCA   To think this girl could mistake my boho chic for
           genuine decay, and that despite my much
           enhanced complexion I was here to... clean?! Pah!

           She looks round.

           I'd presumed if my husband played away he'd be
           in some high-end city John Lewis nightmare hotel,
           cavorting with a paid-up tart. But inconceivably,
           he's crash-landed in this pit of shit. This morning I
           dumped the children on the help, and using the
           tracking app I had secreted on his phone, resolved
           to catch him in the act. For truly I don't care who
           he fumbles, but I must ensure he's careful – I'll be
           damned before I appear the naive wife, who wakes
           one morning to discover pictures of her husband's

errant tongue all splashed across the morning
news. I have investments and aspirations of my
own that needs be served – I'll not rely on him.

'Freddie' eh?

So he's in the bathroom. Well then I could be in
for quite a wait. For despite his lack of hair, he
takes a fucking age.

The buzzer goes. REBECCA *looks around, but no
one comes to answer.*

It rings again and she answers it.

Hello?

TOM   (*Through intercom.*) It's Tom.

REBECCA   Oh er... come up!

She presses the button.

I'll go into this hell, and seek some evidence of
my betrayal. Confrontation smells much sweeter
laced with proof.

She goes off into the rest of the flat.

TOM *appears at the door, a little nervous, with
the bag, dressed in his Harlequin costume.*

He looks around.

TOM   Hello?

No one replies.

(*Aside.*) After my activities last night, I feel
enlivened with a new boldness. Never have I
clicked so much as with Phoebe. Although she did
abandon me and dance with someone else, I do
believe with my fresh confidence I can win her
round. At parties since the plague all must leave
their address in case, and this was Phoebe's...

Hello? Someone let me in...?

He looks around a little.

I'll wait and read, and see who comes.

He sits, with the bag on his lap.

He goes to take out his book. Instead he finds some lipstick.

This is not my book.

He takes out some tights.

This not my gloves.

He takes out a purse.

Nor this my wallet.

He opens the purse.

A name is writ on this card – Lady Susan Climber! This is her bag not mine! They look so similar. Well I must return it swiftly –

He reaches in and gets –

My phone! A silver lining to the cloud.

He notices something in the wallet.

And – this photograph. 'Tis Lady Climber but unlike how I've ever seen her!

He looks closely, shocked.

It makes no sense… but there's only one conclusion… My gosh! If people knew…

PHOEBE   Whose purse is that?

            PHOEBE *has reappeared at the door, her bag now full of eco-friendly cleaning products. She's eating chocolate.*

TOM   Oh.

PHOEBE   Tom! Why are you here? Please don't mistake my surprise, it's a delight to see you, but you're sitting in my flat most uninvited and going through a lady's purse…

TOM   Oh I… found it, and wondered –

PHOEBE   You… ah – I know!

            Taking it from him, including the photo.

TOM   No – wait –

PHOEBE   It must have been Rebecca's, the cleaner, she's
            just arrived. I assume she's gone off to start in the
            kitchen.

            She puts it in with the cleaning things.

            I'll make sure she gets it back. Rebecca! Rebecca!

            The door of the bathroom opens and MATT
            *appears, a towel wrapped round his waist,
            shocked.*

MATT   Why are you calling Rebecca?

PHOEBE   It's the cleaner's name.

MATT   The cleaner?

PHOEBE   Yes I ordered a cleaner, and you know it was so
            strange, only twenty minutes later, she turned up.

MATT   What did she look like?

PHOEBE   Oh typical cleaner, you know, tied-up brown hair,
            shabby jeans, messy T-shirt.

            (*Shouts.*) Rebecca?!

MATT   Rebecca?! It's not the cleaner but my bloody wife!

PHOEBE   What?

MATT   She can't find me here!

TOM   Why not?

PHOEBE   Yes why not just tell her the truth?

REBECCA   (*From offstage.*) Coming!

MATT   You mean just… tell her that really I've had these
            feelings but only acted on them secretly because
            my upbringing kept me repressed, and now, despite
            the trouble it will cause, I'm actually really *happy*

exploring who I really am, sexually and politically, and that I'd love to work with her to find a solution to our future that means we can *all* thrive?

PHOEBE   Exactly!

REBECCA   (*From offstage.*) My god this place is *disgusting*.

MATT   No way!

MATT dives behind the convenient screen, the exact second REBECCA enters. The other two stand as innocently as possible. PHOEBE's still eating chocolate.

REBECCA   What?

PHOEBE   Nothing. Hi.

TOM   Hello.

Beat.

PHOEBE   I got the cleaning items you require.

She holds out the bag. REBECCA doesn't take them.

And also in there is your purse.

REBECCA   I've got my purse here.

PHOEBE   You... Oh.

She takes it back out.

Must be someone else's then. How strange...?

She puts the bag down. REBECCA inspects the bathroom.

REBECCA   Where is he? Your guest that was using the bathroom?

PHOEBE   Oh, I... don't know. Tom did you see –

TOM   Not sure.

REBECCA looks at them.

REBECCA   Hm. Given the smell, I can't stay here much longer, so I'll reveal the truth to you disgusting young people. Quite obviously, I am not the *cleaner*, but Rebecca De Souza MBA DPhil, of the Somerset De Souzas I'm sure you're aware of us. I am currently looking for my husband, who I believe may have, for reasons beyond understanding, spent the night here. His name is Matthew Eton, he's Secretary of State for Procurement.

PHOEBE   Oh right. Um… no, we've not seen him.

REBECCA   He wasn't your visitor, that you spoke about?

TOM   I've only just arrived so –

PHOEBE   He… No.

REBECCA   Because this is his wallet and phone.

            She holds them up, and starts looking through his phone.

            I wanted to say to him that if it is simply that he is sleeping with someone else he need not worry, for I have had multiple affairs and am currently happily riding my lifecoach Paul. So it's not a substantial problem, we just need to coordinate diaries.

PHOEBE   Oh really?! Well that's wonderful news I'm sure he'd love to hear that the marriage will survive. For the sake of the children if nothing else.

REBECCA   Yes, exactly, so all his deception was completely –

            Wait – what's this? A draft email? 'I'm afraid I must tender my resignation from the Conservative Party because I have unexpectedly become a… a…'

            She fumes.

            My god! The snivelling treacherous bastard! Where is he?!

PHOEBE   Oh, well –

REBECCA   *Where?!* One last chance.

PHOEBE   Um...

           Both their eyes go to the screen. Without saying a
           word, REBECCA *looks at it and understands.*

REBECCA   Matthew?

           No answers. She kicks the screen.

           Matthew.

MATT   Hi.

REBECCA   Good morning?

MATT   Not bad so far.

REBECCA   You want to come out?

MATT   Not really.

REBECCA   Is this true? That's you've become a Socialist?

MATT

REBECCA   *Matthew.*

MATT   Um yes. Yes that's right.

REBECCA   Then I'm divorcing you.

MATT   Fair enough. Makes sense. Absolutely.

REBECCA   And you're having the kids.

           MATT *moans.*

MATT   Oh come on / Rebecca –

REBECCA   No no, don't complain. I never wanted them. All
           your idea, to boost your Conservative values, or
           whatever you said. So. Your problem. Yes?

           Yes?

MATT   Yes fine.

REBECCA   Alright. I'll tell the nanny. Divorce will be in the
           post next couple of weeks. I'll leave you to your
           comrades.

MATT   Righty-ho.

              She smiles.

REBECCA   Right! Glad that's all cleared up. Must dash. Got a
              stonker of an article to write. All about some
              absolute dick of a turncoat MP.

              (*To* PHOEBE.) Honestly darling, you don't need a
              cleaner. Bloody fumigator.

PHOEBE   I agree! Farewell!

              REBECCA *goes.*

              We hear the door slam, and then MATT *appears,
              in the towel.*

PHOEBE   Sorry.

MATT   No it's fine I'll just send them to boarding school.

PHOEBE   I meant about your wife.

MATT   Oh! No. Not a problem. Don't need her now, see,
              do I? Freddie!

              FREDDIE *enters, ready for work.* MATT *picks up
              his phone.*

              Labour MPs don't require wives and children.
              Quite the opposite these days.

FREDDIE   Labour MP? You're going to –

MATT   Yes! I've always been known as an astute political
              operative. Carpe that diem! Ride the zeitgeist!

              He presses on the phone.

              There! Sent! Yes! And once dressed, I'll write to
              Sir Keir.

FREDDIE   Keir Starmer?

MATT   That's the chap! Good egg. So. Got to head out.
              Need a new outfit. I might grow a beard...? But
              Freddie, let's meet later? We could... oh... what's
              this?

He sees an invitation on his phone.

Sir Dennis Hedge's Business Awards. How prestigious! Freddie, you must accompany me. I'll text you. Excellent!

He strides out of the room.

PHOEBE   So all is well. You've taken a most abhorrent man and corrected the errors of his ways.

FREDDIE   Yes... Maybe. Anyway, I... er... I should get to work.

TOM   Work? What do you do?

FREDDIE   (*Without much enthusaism.*) Oh I... actually it genuinely is very interesting but I doubt you'll be –

PHOEBE   (*Still holding the purse.*) If not hers, then whose is this?

FREDDIE   Okay.

            FREDDIE *goes as she opens the purse and takes out the photo.*

TOM   Young Phoebe, I think perhaps I should explain, there's been a series of events that seem quite strange, but in looking at that photo –

PHOEBE   Oh how odd! This purse – it must belong to my brother.

TOM   Your brother?

PHOEBE   Jack. Yes, I did visit in disguise to test his character.

TOM   Right...

PHOEBE   And now I see it's his, for he carries within a photo of our long-departed mother. I have one similar. Her face is slightly obscured, sadly as in all the ones we have, but still you see her dark hair, and how she holds her babies tenderly. By all accounts she was the most loving and natural

mother, keen for us to be the best, all before she
died of course in that bizarre and sudden accident
at the zoo.

Ah. If only I could speak to her! I wonder if the
trauma of our parents both so lost like this, could
explain young Jack's descent to hell, and indeed,
perhaps my own virtuous obsessions? But no –
they're gone. And we must manage the best we
can... sorry I am still drunk and weepy but I...
I have to go! In truth I can't bear my brother being
out there in the cold, alone. I must find him, and
save him!

TOM   Phoebe, I have news.

PHOEBE   You do?

TOM   Indeed but before we talk I think that you should
            dress, and I must too. If I can borrow clothes,
            we'll go for coffee. For with what I can reveal,
            your world will turn on its head and you should
            not, I think, be off your face but cold as stone.

            PHOEBE *looks ill.*

            You okay?

PHOEBE   Indeed not.
            For though I crave to know what it's about
            I first must go, and let this mass of vomit out.

            She goes. TOM *goes after her, holding up his
            phone.*

ACT FIVE

Scene One

Sir Dennis Hedge's house. Kensington. Big and expensive.

SIR DENNIS *enters with* HANNAH.

SIR D.   My gratitude for taking on the arrangements today
            with such zeal.

HANNAH   A pleasure sir, I will be in my element.

SIR D.   I'm certain of that, and yet, as I look at all these
            honorific guests and entrepreneurial celebrants, I
            feel a gap. They excel at business, but which of
            them does truly feel responsibility unto the world?

HANNAH   I wonder sir, if you have expectations too high?
            Our age is one of the individual self, is it not?
            Self-fulfilment, self-image.

SIR D.   But what of the current activism amongst the
            young! That's genuine, isn't it?

            HANNAH *laughs*.

HANNAH   Oh sir! Nay! 'Tis but the fashion! They'll do it if it's
            easy – they claim their motivation is the betterment
            of society but this is clearly false. The vast majority
            are possessed by the same motivations as every
            young person in history – money, pleasure, respect
            and sex. There's few who'll actually sacrifice
            anything in their life for a larger goal.

SIR D.   If true then what you say would crush my soul. So
            you may hold your bleak opinion, but I'll remain
            in hope.

HANNAH   Well bless you for that Sir Dennis. We need
            deluded optimists.

SIR D.   And what of jaded cynics Ms Tweetwell? Do we
            need them too?

            A moment.

            Will you stay here to welcome guests, I must
            withdraw to attend the hall.

            SIR DENNIS *goes.*

HANNAH   (*Aside.*) I wish I could share that hope, like I used
            to, but he is correct that I now live as a ruthless
            cynic; alone, without love, passion, or joy. And all
            because of Lady Climber!

            JACK *enters. He is dishevelled, tired-looking, and
            wet from the rain.*

            Oh! No – sorry, the homeless shelter's round the
            corner, I'm sure they'll help you out.

JACK   Ms Tweetwell, 'tis I, young Jack.

HANNAH   Young… Oh god, yes… I now perceive between
            the matted hair and encrusted dirt a human being
            but why, after your disgrace last night have you
            come here? And muddied my pristine floor with
            your besodden sole?

JACK   Last evening I was not myself. For reasons I do not
            understand, I have been seeing visions of Death –
            It's made me… lose my way. Today when I awoke,
            within a skip, I decided I must apologise. I am most
            sorry for causing such a commotion. For spouting
            those beliefs was inconsiderate and something you
            would never be associated with. But now I pledge
            my leaf has turned and I beseech your forgiveness,
            that we may rekindle what we started.

HANNAH   It matters little what you believe, but that which
            you present. You must learn discretion.

            I propose a test. You'll be my helper here today.
            If you can indeed stick to my script, and welcome
            all and sundry with tact and good humour, maybe,
            I will consider a recoupling.

JACK   An offer fairer than my wildest dreams.

HANNAH   Then good. Go hence, you'll find the waiters'
            dressing room. Exchange your clothes, spray some
            Lynx, then return forthwith.

JACK   My thanks indeed. I shall, in haste, ablute.

            He goes.

HANNAH   (*Aside.*) How strange it is that he returns, and what
            is more, that I do not reject him out of hand! There
            is a soft spot there. As if I crave something...

            Enter AUNTY JULIE, *pretending to be posh.
            Badly.*

JULIE   The goodest of mornings.

HANNAH   Greetings madam, do you have an invitation?

JULIE   I do most certainly indeedy, for here it is most
            readily on my telephone.

HANNAH   Right.

            AUNTY JULIE *shows it to* HANNAH.

JULIE   I have it with well authority indeed from a source
            most authoritised that Lady Susan Climber will be
            most in attendance here today.

HANNAH   Er – Indeed but she is yet to arrive.

JULIE   Ah right. I mean – Indeed. Then shall I wait within
            this very parlour?

HANNAH   Why no, perhaps just head through there, and
            she'll arrive soon. I'll let her know you're here,
            Mrs –

AYN JULIE. Miss, actually. Miss... Aunty Julie.

HANNAH   I'll let her know you asked Miss Julie.

JULIE   My bestest thanks.

            AUNTY JULIE *goes into the party.*

HANNAH   (*Aside*.) So sad. These clearly northern women
           deceive no one.

           JACK *appears from another door, now dressed as*
           a waiter, and scrubbed up amazingly well.

           Well that's a difference in but two minutes.

JACK   Lynx body spray is wondrous magic in a can.

HANNAH   Indeed, but now I must admit you to my greatest
           secret. It is a scheme I have in place that I will get
           such pleasure from myself, but now you're here I
           suspect I'll draw a double pleasure from it shared.

JACK   What scheme?

HANNAH   For reasons you need not be aware, I harbour a
           resentful wound from Lady Climber, and in
           forging closure I must get some cold revenge.

JACK   I see.

HANNAH   I have become her social media consultant and
           made her believe she can succeed through causing
           outrage. As such, she senses all that she desires is
           within her grasp. But today, just as she reaches up
           to lay her hands upon her prize, I'll make her
           stretch too far, and bring her crashing down.

JACK   How?

HANNAH   Inflated with success and most trusting in my
           advice, she attends these awards today, and will be
           seen by all the most influential people in London.
           However, I have also advised her what to *wear*
           and ensured it is so massively offensive that the
           moment she appears, she will be forever disgraced
           by every side, and eradicated from society. With
           this story forever in the memory and online, she
           will be unable to work, unable to thrive, unable to
           live any meaningful life from this day forward.

JACK   What she must have done to you, to bring revenge
           like this!

HANNAH   You've no idea.

JACK   Tell me what costume you proscribed?

She looks round and whispers it in JACK*'s ear.*

My god.

LADY C.   (*From offstage.*) You've got my details, put it on account!

HANNAH   Ah! 'Tis her. Now do not betray your shock, or laugh, for she must be revealed in front of all.

HANNAH *turns to get ready.*

JACK   (*Aside.*) What Lady Climber did to Tweetwell is a mystery, but hearing this revenge does make me feel this pain inside once more. Could it be a kind of… conscience? For is this vengeance too cruel? I'faith – she comes – I'll push it down again. 'Tis not my business and besides, why should I care for Lady Climber, such an awful, selfish, person?!

LADY CLIMBER *enters, wearing a huge overcoat.* CARSON *is with her, holding her bag.*

LADY C.   No, no Carson just deposit the bag there and go home.

CARSON   But ma'am the taxi has left?

LADY C.   You think I'm made of money? Get the bus.

CARSON   Yes ma'am.

He dodders away.

HANNAH   Lady Climber! How delightful to see you today. But so becovered! Is it raining outside? I didn't hear the patter.

LADY C.   Not raining, but having bedecked myself as instructed, I caught sight of my outfit in the mirror, and perceived I looked… provocative. Before I wore it publicly, I was keen to check I had understood.

HANNAH   And hence the largest coat I've ever seen. Pray
           turn and let me see. I will set your mind at rest.

           *LADY CLIMBER turns so she's facing away from
           us, and opens up the coat so that only HANNAH
           can see. LADY CLIMBER looks away and misses
           HANNAH's slightly shocked and then joyful
           reaction.*

           Oh well! It's – Hmm – yes, it's all I desired, and
           more. After this, your reputation will be most
           assured.

LADY C.   You're certain?

HANNAH   If you require further assurance, perhaps you'll
           permit my young associate here his opinion? If
           Jack approves then you may wear it proud, with
           double confidence.

LADY C.   Hmm. Indeed, he may behold.

           *HANNAH gestures to JACK to come and have a
           look.*

           *He braces himself, but when he sees, his eyebrows
           rise. It's quite a sight.*

           Crucially though, he doesn't laugh.

           Is it not… too much?

JACK   Why…

           (*Aside.*) Oh what to say. This feeling in me grows.
           Why am I unable to pursue my desire without this
           sickness in my gut?

           No! Not too much. 'Tis perfect. Argh!

HANNAH   You see!

           *JACK winces in pain. LADY CLIMBER closes
           the coat.*

           So throw the coat away! And stand your tallest.

           But JACK's squirming.

LADY C.   What's wrong with him?

HANNAH   He's shy.

LADY C.   I despise the shy.

HANNAH   Jack go somewhere else.

JACK   Yes, I shall!

He goes out.

HANNAH   You rightly hate the bashful, then Lady Climber, be not shy yourself!

LADY C.   Yes. Hmm. Perhaps I'll wear it here, within this room, to begin. Since it's only you and I...

She's about to open the coat, when AUNTY JULIE *enters, holding a glass of champagne.*

JULIE   Hello sis!

She sees LADY CLIMBER *and bursts out laughing.*

Wow! Big coat!

LADY C.   What on earth are you doing here?

JULIE   Why are you dressed like that?

LADY C.   Fashion.

JULIE   What's underneath?

HANNAH   This is your sister, Lady Climber?

LADY C.   Unfortunately. Why are you here?

JULIE   I'll tell you, if you'll reveal first.

LADY C.   Oh for christ's sake. Tweetwell this had better be worth the effort.

HANNAH   It shall I promise you.

LADY C.   Very well. Come.

AUNTY JULIE stands in the right place (upstage).
LADY CLIMBER reveals the costume to her.

AUNTY JULIE *screams*.

JULIE   Christ!

LADY C.   I should have known your opinion would be
            fruitless.

JULIE   No I mean... well, sister, you might think it's...
            funny, dressing like this. But / have you
            considered the implications?

HANNAH   Lady Climber let me ensure the crowd is gathered
            for your entrance. 'Twould be a shame if such a
            glorious impact was missed...

            She goes.

LADY C.   Oh why am I discussing this with you – something
            too sophisticated for your provincial mind to
            comprehend. Just tell me why you've left your
            region.

JULIE   I'm here to *warn* you! For though you treat me
            with contempt and never show much love, you
            remain my sister. You should know young
            Phoebe's come to London, as well as Jack. I'd
            thought it was okay as London is so huge it should
            prevent your meeting. But then Phoebe texted me
            that she was attending a party for Netclix –

LADY C.   Netflix.

JULIE   Netbix, and suddenly I thought perhaps you might
            be there. Unable to make contact with anyone,
            I came myself, put on a costume and sneaked in.
            I watched and made sure you never met.

LADY C.   You mean the two of them were there all last
            night? Oh. My stomach turns.

JULIE   Indeed and they're moving even closer I believe.
            For instance Jack was with Ms Tweetwell, and
            she's now in your employ, am I right?

LADY C.   Jack? There was a young man called Jack here just
            now.

JULIE   Yes that may be him! Didn't you recognise him?

LADY C.   Why should I? Last I saw him he was but six
           months.

JULIE   But all the pictures that I sent...?

LADY C.   Made excellent kindling in my wood-burning
           stove – so that was Jack!

JULIE   My sister we must tell them! For they are grown,
           will make no demands, and even though you wish
           it not the case you are their mother and –

LADY C.   No! The deal we made in those prenatal days
           remains in blood. I would, despite my instinct,
           give them birth, on condition you would take them
           swift away, that they would never know, and I
           would never hear of them again. To this we will
           adhere like glue.

           HANNAH *enters*.

HANNAH   All is ready. The guests await. And what a flock.
           Matt Eton attends. The Duchess of Cambridge,
           and Steven Bartlett too.

LADY C.   Well then let me get my mirror to ensure all is
           perfection.

           *She reaches into her bag, and takes out a framed
           picture of Ken Loach.*

           But this is not my mirror.

           And now a Mars bar.

           And this not my brush. My god. That boy! He
           took my bag! Which means... he's got his phone
           back and he could... Oh god! Any minute he
           might –

HANNAH   Lady Climber, might what? What ails thee? What
           boy?

LADY C.   I have to go –

           Enter SIR DENNIS.

SIR D.   Miss Tweetwell! The hall grows full, our guests
                are keen, but yet –

                He sees LADY CLIMBER.

                Lady Climber. You're here! And what a large coat.

LADY C.   You never did have any taste.

SIR D.   Before we go another round, please allow a pause.
                I have been concerned your recent assaults are due
                to a deficit of affection. That perhaps I should
                remove our enmity, in the hope you may redeem
                some compassion. Therefore, for whatever harm
                I've done you in the past, forgive me, and let us
                start afresh with renewed respect and *love*.

LADY C.   I think I was just sick in my mouth.

HANNAH   A sincere and wonderful apology Sir Dennis, I am
                sure Lady Climber will reply in kind?

LADY C.   In what?

HANNAH   In *kind*, my lady? We want the afternoon to
                proceed, do we not?

LADY C.   Oh Christ. Alright. If ever I have commented on
                what an utter arsehole you are, then... sorry. I
                should have kept it to myself.

SIR D.   Susan, it's me. I know you live a solitary life and
                for years you have played the antagonist, but you
                don't need to wear that mask.

LADY C.   Mask sir?

                They look at each other. LADY CLIMBER *caught
                out.*

                I don't know what you –

MATT   Ah! Good afternoon!

                MATT *enters. He looks identical to the first half,
                but now with a red tie, rather than blue. He's
                holding a glass of champagne.*

Great to see you. I'm Matt Eton MP, recently divorced, now openly polyamorous. I hope that's okay with everyone here? I say! What a tremendous coat!

LADY C.   I thank you.

HANNAH   Divorced, did you say Mr Eton?

MATT   Indeed, not quite crossed the T's but the I's are firmly dotted.

HANNAH   Then with your newfound liberty you must surely make fresh acquaintance with Lady Climber! She lost you in the crowd last evening and yearned all night.

MATT   All night? Really?

LADY C.   Oh... well... yes. Couldn't help it.

MATT   Blimey.

SIR D.   Excuse me both. I must attend to my guests.

     SIR DENNIS *goes*.

HANNAH   So shall the two of you attend together? What a rich coupling that would be!

LADY C.   Well yes indeed –

HANNAH   And Mr Eton she has much to reveal under that coat I promise.

MATT   Under her... Crikey. Only thing is I was actually looking for a friend called Frederick, but... he seems not to have turned up, sadly. Therefore yes! Lady Climber, if you will have me, you shall yearn no longer.

     He takes her hand.

HANNAH   Lady Climber, now is the moment! Take your entrance with Mr Eton, discard your over-garment, and face the world!

LADY C.   Very well. I shall indeed.

They make to go but suddenly JACK *runs on to stage.*

JACK   Stop!

They all turn to face him.

MATT   Oh god not that annoying boy who ruined the dance. It's all he does. I love dancing so much. I once had this fabulous night in Aberdeen –

JACK   I have to tell Lady Climber something of vital importance. I'm sorry Ms Tweetwell, but for reasons I don't fully understand, I must!

LADY C.   Must tell me what?

JACK   Why that –

PHOEBE   Stop!

They all turn the other way to see PHOEBE *enter, with* TOM – *who's filming everything – and* FREDDIE.

PHOEBE   I have to tell Jack and Lady Climber something of vital importance.

JACK   Phoebe!

PHOEBE   Jack!

FREDDIE   Matt?

MATT   Freddie! Ah.

Realising and dropping LADY CLIMBER's *hand.*

LADY C.   You! Your phone! Give me that phone!

She grabs it from TOM, *as* JACK *continues.*

JACK   Phoebe forgive me but I had news of vital importance I was about to relate when you appeared with also news of – I'm sure – equal vital importance.

PHOEBE   Oh.

JACK	Without knowledge of how vital the relative importances are, how should we proceed?
PHOEBE	Since you were here before, you should go first.
MATT	Freddie shall we go and get a drink?
LADY C.	*No*. Stay here. Will someone get *on* with this?
JACK	Lady Climber for reasons I have not divined you're being tricked by Ms Tweetwell. The clothes you wear are offensive in the extreme, far more than you realise, and will result in your complete rejection by all society.
LADY C.	You mean –
JACK	You'll be left without a penny to your name, and a face that will forever be regarded with horror and disdain.
LADY C.	Ms Tweetwell, is this youth a madman?
HANNAH	My lady really! You would take the word of such a boy as this. A youth of dubious upbringing, only interested in drugs and sex, without a purpose, without a brain, without a moral in his soul.
JULIE	Let me just stop you there! For it was I that raised this boy.
JACK	Aunty Julie?! I didn't recognise you without the straw and dirt.
PHOEBE	Aunty what brings you here?
JULIE	Oh… er… just a holiday! Yes I raised this boy and although he's had his share of sex and drugs, I tell you now, whether he knows it or not, there's conscience strong as steel within his very gut.
JACK	My gut! Well that explains it! The sickness. It was you.
JULIE	I should hope so!
PHOEBE	Oh Jack! You're doing the right thing! At last!

JACK   Lady Climber please – I speak the truth. And I
            here know that what you wear right now is
            incredibly offensive.

FREDDIE   Why? What is it?

MATT   Yes i'faith! How bad can it be?

            They all look at LADY CLIMBER *(she has ended
            up downstage). She then reveals the costume. They
            all gasp, wince, etc. (except* HANNAH*).*

MATT   Holy Moses...

LADY C.   Hmm. A revealing reaction. Ms Tweetwell, I have
            special reason to believe this boy. Tell me your
            scheme immediately.

            A beat.

HANNAH   Alright! It's true. I wanted you to fall and never
            rise again. And I'll tell you why! When I first
            moved to London, I was optimistic, hopeful, and
            intent on a career in television, desperate to
            engage with creative people. But I had no way in,
            until through a chance encounter I secured a
            position on a reality show as a runner. I performed
            my duties to the best of my abilities, but one
            contestant began to place more and more demands
            on me, to fetch her food, make her coffee, to tidy
            up after her miniscule dog. She asked the
            impossible then insulted me for failing. I could put
            up no resistance, as this was my only opportunity,
            but as it progressed she destroyed my self-esteem,
            my passion, my belief in joy itself. She moved on,
            creating a career for herself, full of money and
            acclaim. I retreated, depressed, hid away for two
            years, and then slowly, through social media, built
            a reputation as a consultant, but all that time I had
            one aim: to bring that woman down, as she had
            brought me down. For that show was The
            Apprentice 2015, and that contestant was you
            Lady Climber. You showed no mercy.

A suitable moment to let that land. Then –

LADY C. Is that *it*?! Jesus darling. We all start at the bottom. My life has been one setback after another and I tell you, none of it was fair, and yet I hold no grudge 'gainst anyone. *Move on.* Now, Mr Eton shall we –

JULIE But sister, surely, on hearing this story, you must want to apologise?

HANNAH 'No grudge'! A barefaced lie! You harbour one of the most famous enmities in London!

LADY C. You mean Sir Dennis? Yes, we have quarrelled much, but –

TOM And you seemed pretty upset this morning.

MATT This morning? What / happened this morning?

LADY C. (*Shutting him up.*) Uh! Uh! Let's not get into that.

JACK What reason?

LADY C. I beg your pardon?

JACK You said that you had special reason to believe in me. What could it be? For we have never met.

LADY C. Oh just your... face.

PHOEBE Lady Climber, forgive me, but as you well know, you have met this boy indeed, but not for years.

LADY C. Who are *you*? My god this is getting convoluted.

PHOEBE I'm Phoebe to his Jack. Brought up by Aunty Julie here, upon the 'pparent death of our dear mother at the zoo one day. Victim to a herd of rhinos.

MATT Rhinos?

JULIE I was thinking on my feet.

PHOEBE But this is not the truth, is it Aunty? Our mother lives. And brother – this is her purse.

She holds up the purse.

LADY C.   Give that back.

PHOEBE   Within, most treasured, the owner keeps a picture
          you will recognise.

          She holds up a small picture.

          Our young mother with us as babes in her arms.

          That mother stands before us.

          They turn and face LADY CLIMBER.

LADY C.   Oh, *fine.* This is something I had hoped to avoid.
          Certainly I could have done without the *audience.*
          But yes. Hi. I'm your mum.

          They stare at her. JACK *takes a step towards her.*

JACK   Mother...?

LADY C.   (*Shooing.*) No, no.

PHOEBE   But why, if you were alive, and young, and
          beautiful, did you give us up?

JULIE   Oh because she was so poor! There wasn't any
          chance she could –

LADY C.   Stop it Julie. You two want the truth?

JACK   I'faith of course.

PHOEBE   With all my racing heart.

LADY C.   Why do they speak like that?

JULIE   You said to bring them up well. That's what you
          said.

LADY C.   Yes. Well. Not... weird.

          She turns to PHOEBE *and* JACK.

          I didn't want you, because, quite simply, I had
          other things I wanted to do. I would have taken
          measures, except Julie said she'd have you
          instead. So eight months, and one Caesarean later,
          off you went, and I was never supposed to hear
          from you again.

PHOEBE   Except we weren't completely extinguished in your heart, for there I found, this photograph in your purse.

LADY C.   Indeed it's true I carry it by my side both day and night.

JACK   Then you've *not* forgot! There's still some modicum of love!

LADY C.   You misunderstand. The photo is the very best contraception. If I've missed a pill, or if we have no condom there to hand, but I am keen and tempted to take a chance, just one look at that photo of the two of you, and whatever lustful fire in me dies at once.

MATT   (*Almost to himself.*) That's a jolly good idea.

PHOEBE   So… you are not pleased to see us? I had thought whilst coming here, that when you met us, you'd realise that your desperation for respect and wealth was compensation for your loss. I had assumed that given a chance to have a family, you'd find a warmer, more fulfilled and valuable happiness, than you would ever find in your world of money, sex and power.

LADY C.   You thought all women secretly need to be mothers to be fulfilled?

PHOEBE   I… Oh. No, that's an offensive thought, I agree.

JACK   And what of our father?

LADY C.   What have you been told? Terminated by a flock of geese?

JULIE   Don't be silly!

PHOEBE   A runaway milkfloat.

JULIE   That was in the local paper. That actually happened!

LADY C.   Alright. Alright. Well let's get it *all* out then – he isn't dead.

PHOEBE   Not dead?

LADY C.   Your father and I were close, but then had a severe
            disagreement, and the next day I found I was
            pregnant. Because it wasn't his business I never
            enlightened him. And I've been in a feud with him
            ever since.

PHOEBE   This man – do you have a name?

HANNAH   A feud? Then you mean the father is –

            The door opens and SIR DENNIS *enters.*

SIR D.   Well! Here you all are! Come come we're on the
            verge of starting the – But why are you in a line like
            this, with mouths as guppies? Is there something
            wrong with my appearance? I highly doubt it...

PHOEBE   No sir, indeed, your appearance is most welcome.

SIR D.   Good.

PHOEBE   Father!

            She runs and hugs him.

SIR D.   Er. I think you've made a slight mistake.

JACK   Indeed no. My name is Jack, this Phoebe.

SIR D.   How odd, the names I would have given my own
            children, had I ever had them. Which I didn't, but
            so keenly wish I did.

JACK   We are those children sir. You are our father.

SIR D.   ...but how? I mean you must be what, twenty-two
            years old, and the only woman I was with back
            then was... Lady Climber, and she hasn't –

LADY C.   Dennis sorry, I popped them out and off, to my
            sister here.

(JULIE   Hi. It's really good to meet you!

SIR D.   Good afternoon.)

LADY C.   Neither of us wanted children, but either way, here
            they are: Fully furnished. No harm done!

SIR D.   My girl, and boy... What wonders! What darlings!
            So young and full of hope. Just as I imagined!

LADY C.   Good! Have a wonderful life. Now, Mr Eton shall
            we –

MATT   Freddie, my love, do you fancy these awards?
            Shall we go together? Hit the bar?

LADY C.   Freddie? Who's –

FREDDIE   Yes I... I will go to the party, indeed.

MATT   Excellent!

FREDDIE   But not with you.

MATT   You... But I... I have done all you asked! We
            made most glorious love, then I listened, learned,
            about how my ideology was incorrect. I then
            resigned, changed parties and now lead the fight
            from the opposite benches. What more could you
            want?

FREDDIE   What more could I want?

MATT   Yes, for surely now the fence between us is
            removed and we may joyously proceed!

FREDDIE   What more could I *want*?

            Why penance, sir.

            Grace.

            You were minister in the pandemic, while
            dispensing strict regulation locking us down, and
            while many thousands lay dying, you ignored your
            own law, partied in the garden, had gross relations,
            and gave lucrative contracts to your friends –

MATT   Freddie, most of that's unproven –

FREDDIE   So if truly now you see the errors of your ways,
            then you would not effortless flip to more power
            and position but instead find some method... to...

            Apologise.

Make amends.

That man I might accompany. But not this.

MATT   Oh ho ho! Well this is fine comedy!

Silence.

I... I'm a good man.

Am I not?

Am I not?

No one agrees. He starts ripping his red tie off.

Well fine! I do all this and what thanks do I get?!
You know what? Forget the whole, bloody, *thing*.
I'm going back where I belong. True blue. Pretend
I'm happy. Business deals, with my mates. Sorted.
And I may be *selfish* or whatever, and in denial
about... well quite a lot admittedly – but at least
unlike you doomsters and gloomsters, I'm
optimistic about the future.

Well... my future anyway. I'm going back to the
party. My *real* friends.

So! I think that's it. Great to see you. Thanks very
much.

MATT *leaves.*

FREDDIE   I must go too. So much to do.

He leaves.

SIR D.   The awards will be beginning soon. We must in
             haste. Lady Climber?

LADY C.   Absolutely. Let me just remove the coat...

ALL   What?! / No! / Don't! (*Etc.*)

She stops and looks at them.

LADY C.   Why shouldn't I?

SIR D.   Why not?

PHOEBE   Mother you know the reason! Ms Tweetwell made you –

LADY C.   She did *not* make me do anything. She *suggested* it. Despite Ms Tweetwell's dubious motives, I see no reason I should be cowed.

SIR D.   What *are* you all talking about? What could possibly be under the coat that –

AUNTY JULIE *whispers to him.*

My god! Lady Climber! The woman that you were when we first met would never have considered such a thing.

ROSALIND *enters, out of breath, and marches straight up to* TOM.

ROSALIND   *There* you are! Thank goodness I put that application on your phone and tracked you down. My god look at the state of you. What's happened?

TOM   Everything!

ROSALIND   What does that mean?

TOM   I smoked!

ROSALIND   What?

TOM   And got drunk!

ROSALIND   Got *what*?!

TOM   And slept with someone. Oh Mother you never told me the joy!

ROSALIND   Who? Who did you sleep with?

TOM *looks at* LADY CLIMBER, *pleading.*

TOM   I... er... .

Everyone slowly also looks at LADY CLIMBER.

LADY C.   Oh, alright. Yes. Again. Over here.

She gives the phone back to TOM.

ROSALIND You?

LADY C.   Yes.

PHOEBE   Mum!

LADY C.   *Stop*.

ROSALIND Lady Climber. Well. Did you enjoy it?

LADY C.   As a matter of fact, I did.

ROSALIND Hmm.

She turns to her son.

Did you enjoy it Tom?

TOM   Immensely.

ROSALIND Hmm.

She looks LADY CLIMBER *up and down.*

Why are you wearing such a large coat?

TOM *whispers in her ear. She looks shocked.*

Oh! You don't hold back do you? Unafraid to push the boundaries of good taste and shake the cage. Well! I am totally outraged Lady Climber. I mean, properly *offended*… and I love it! What television it will be! We should get you two series greenlit straight off the bat with this. Frankly, I'm pleased my son has such good taste. And I have to say it's broken the spell. Tom, you may move out and commence your life! Lady Climber you are forgiven, and if you ever want to see to my son again –

TOM   Wait –

ROSALIND – you are *most* welcome.

TOM   Eeeewww! Mum!

ROSALIND Lady Climber, you're a star. Call me, and we will make a huge success.

ROSALIND *goes, leaving the door open.*

LADY C.   Ah! You see? She adores it!

SIR D.   I beg of you don't go out there –

JULIE   Please!

JACK   You will regret it, you know not the harm it will cause. The hurt!

CARSON *enters, through the now open door.*

CARSON   And for what it's worth, I've been listening hard at the keyhole, and would also advise against it.

LADY C.   Oh you miserable –

PHOEBE   Mum, please –

CARSON   Mum?

PHOEBE   – it would destroy everything, cause offence to all, and mean that all this hope for happiness was –

LADY C.   Stop! It's *my choice*!

Look at you all!

I don't want a family. I never have. To be bonded without option to strangers from birth. Responsibility with no power? Love with no escape? 'Tis not for me. Indeed, I desire success. I adore my ambition. Of this I remain most proud.

'Tis true Sir Dennis. I am alone. But there are worse things.

To rely on a mother who manifests only cruelty, then abandonment. Or a father who insulted us nightly, then spent his money on drink, rather than his children. Who as I grew, came back every few years, with his insults and attitude, yet begged me to support him. Which I *do* to this very day. When I was still a child, cowering, hungry, looking after my sister on a cold night, I made a pledge I would never rely on anyone.

Perhaps money and power and status wouldn't bring me happiness. But I made my decision, and since then they've been more constant than family. A firmer friend, than friends.

Julie found her solace in community. I found mine in cash.

But surely, if I have *any* freedom, then I'm allowed to make that choice.

Yes?

None of them answer. The silence indicating their begrudging agreement.

LADY CLIMBER *turns to* HANNAH.

Ms Tweetwell, all I say is true. But it does not excuse my behaviour to you.

I... apologise.

HANNAH   Thank you Lady Climber. And I in turn apologise for the horrific obscenity that you currently wear beneath that coat.

LADY C.   Oh my dear! Apologise not...

For under this coat is a glory. And a glory the impact of which should be more public than those petty awards.

I shall not be told what to do, not be told who I am. Not by *you*. Not by my *family*. Not by anyone.

She turns to face us. The family gathered, watching, upstage.

Let me turn to this window, overlooking the packed square.

Let me stand, and gather their attention.

Ah! They look up! Expecting magnificence. Huddled together, so tired of monotony.

Let me look them in the eye, before I act for their freedom.

And for my infamy. For this moment will be forever spoken of. In outrage, in myth. The day I took the coat *off*.

Because I could.

She unties the coat.

And the world changed.

Because it must.

She grasps hold of the edge of the coat.

No apology for offence. 'Tis the nature of the world.

Brace yourself kids!

She looks at us. Judges the crowd.

A moment of what? Compassion? Does she see something in us? In our desire? In our warning?

She does the coat up.

Maybe tomorrow.

Carson?

She leaves. CARSON follows – as he does, he turns to PHOEBE, JACK and AUNTY JULIE.

He stares at them for a moment. A tear in his eye…

CARSON   Farewell.

          Then –

LADY C.   (*From offstage.*) *Carson!*

PHOEBE   Goodbye sir.

JACK   Farewell.

          He turns and goes.

JULIE   Well. Don't know about you lot but I could do with a drink. Sir Dennis, if you want a glass or

two of that free wine with me, I wouldn't object.
You remind me a lot of my postman. We have
wonderful sex, him and I. I bet we would too!
Come find me if you fancy it. See you later kids!

She goes, leaving SIR DENNIS, PHOEBE, JACK,
TOM *and* HANNAH.

SIR D.   Well! My children! I –

            JENNY *suddenly enters –*

JENNY   Phoebe! You left without a word!

PHOEBE   Jenny! I had to – it was urgent. And I didn't think
            you'd care. You said people come and go in your
            flat. That sex doesn't mean anything except
            pleasure.

JENNY   Yeah, well. It was really good but not meaningless.
            You've learnt from me, and I've learnt from you.
            I've decided I'll steal no longer. Instead I thought
            I'd come here and honestly convince these young
            entrepreneurs of the debase nature of capitalism. I
            hoped we might do that... together.

            PHOEBE *kisses her.*

PHOEBE   Jenny! Go forth into the party, and I will see you
            in a moment.

JENNY   Alright. Don't be long!

            She goes. A moment then –

SIR D.   Well! My children! I never –

TOM   Your heart is with another?

PHOEBE   Oh Tom. Not just my heart. I believe my loins as
            well.

TOM   I understand, of course. I suppose I'll just have to
            seek a connection... elsewhere.

            He gets his things together as HANNAH *turns to*
            JACK.

HANNAH   I must go too. Jack?

JACK   Yes?

HANNAH   Call me.

JACK   With pleasure.

                As TOM *makes to go* HANNAH *passes him.*

HANNAH   So, you've got all this on film?

TOM   What? Oh, yeah. I thought I'd make a
                documentary about my experiences in London.

HANNAH   But why? Who would buy it?

TOM   Oh I wouldn't do it for money. Just… to make
                something…

HANNAH   You mean… oh… Well might I… help you? I'd
                like to learn to do… something, just for… joy?

TOM   Sure.

HANNAH   (*Holding her hand out.*) Hannah Tweetwell.

TOM   Tom Double-Budget, but I'm changing the name.

HANNAH   Good idea.

                She takes TOM *off. As they go –*

TOM   I lost my virginity today.

HANNAH   That's nice.

                They go. SIR DENNIS *turns to* PHOEBE *and*
                JACK.

SIR D.   Well! My children! I had been looking for an heir.
                Someone truly worthy of my riches. Who would
                have thought I'd find them of my very own blood?

JACK   You mean we will inherit some money?

SIR D.   A fortune Jack! You'll never have to work again.

JACK   Most wonderful news!

                He doubles up in pain.

                Oh but… This sickness!

PHOEBE   I think I know the cause. Sir Dennis, you were
           looking for someone young to invest in, who had
           ideas, and passions to improve the world?

SIR D.   Indeed that was my plan but surely now there's
           you two –

PHOEBE   Sir 'tis neither right nor fair that we, who have
           done nothing to earn that wealth, should be given
           it simply as we share your blood. The moral thing
           would be for us to make our way ourselves.

JACK   Well hang on Phoebe let's not be too hasty, surely
           we could –

           The pain again.

           Ow!

SIR D.   What is the matter with him?

PHOEBE   He fights his nature sir. Despite the recent months
           his is a good soul, and it is finally rebelling 'gainst
           his debauchery. Jack this only will get worse the
           more you resist. Be good, and all will be well!

JACK   What? No sex, no drugs, no fun!

PHOEBE   Jack, I had sex most extraordinary last night, and
           drugs and so much fun, but do you see my
           conscience twisted thus? Why no, for what we do
           in private sexually with full consent, how much
           we drink, or smoke, to ourselves, and what we
           wear and say, are our decisions. We must have that
           freedom or we have no life. I agree! But with that
           freedom, as we have the most exciting lives, and
           try things out, and get things wrong, and *fail all
           the time*, and forgive failure in others, why not
           also try, just try, to be *good*.

           JACK *looks at her. Relaxed, and undoubled.*

           Dear Jack. Listen to your heart.

JACK   Well… my heart says that… due to the link
           between capitalism and climate change, the

present hope that technology will solve the problem is misplaced, and actually it's going to take turning away from capitalist-based consumerism to something more like a sharing economy, something that more resembles – oh –

Oh!

I feel better!

He nods, thoughtfully. Then turns to SIR DENNIS.

Father, keep your money. We'll work the future out ourselves.

SIR D.   I know you will. I'll keep my finance to myself, but it warms my heart to know that young people such as you exist. Who are aware the world is complicated, yet preserve your generation's passion for change.

FREDDIE enters.

FREDDIE   Oo. Sorry. Left my hat.

He collects it, and is on his way out.

PHOEBE   Freddie I've been meaning to ask, what *do* you do for a living?

FREDDIE   Oh I co-founded a charity. We work in the East End with young people from disadvantaged and marginalised backgrounds, and help them to develop skills, start businesses, get involved in the sectors they want, you know, all that. We're doing well, but we struggle to match the demand.

I mean, what we really need is a big injection of money. But that's not likely, is it? Especially at the moment.

SIR DENNIS look at him.

SIR D.   What's your name young man?

FREDDIE   Freddie Peripheral.

SIR D.   Well Peripheral no longer! Let's you and I talk.
                I might be able to help.

FREDDIE   Oh. Alright. Thanks!

JACK   Father, go and talk now with Freddie at the party.
                Phoebe and I must have a moment, and then we
                shall attend.

SIR D.   Very well. Young man? Let's make some plans.

                They go. PHOEBE *and* JACK *are left with each
                other onstage.*

                They hug, then turn out.

JACK   My sister, now I see what I had missed
                While having sex and gambling pissed
                That though we need to live most free
                Our freedom needs responsibility.

PHOEBE   Oh Jack I suppose in truth that's mostly right
                But generalising sounds so fucking trite
                For rules, like twins, or rhymes, can't hold
                When life's at large and living bold
                Instead tell stories, complex tales
                Where virtue wins but sometimes fails.
                And always listen to what scandals say
                They whisper if we live, then we must *play.*

                Glorious music. Ticker tape. Fireworks.

                Curtain.

                End of play.